YALE

&

THE IVY LEAGUE CARTEL

How a college lost its soul and became a hedge fund

YALE

&

THE IVY LEAGUE CARTEL

How a college lost its soul and became a hedge fund

EDWIN S. ROCKEFELLER

PUBLISHED BY FIDELI PUBLISHING INC.

Copyright © 2015 by Edwin S. Rockefeller

Yale & The Ivy League Cartel
Paperback – published 2015 Fideli Publishing Inc.
ISBN: 978-1-60414-872-5

Publisher's Cataloging-in-Publication

Rockefeller, Edwin S., author.
　　Yale & the Ivy League cartel : how a college lost its soul and became a hedge fund / Edwin S. Rockefeller.
　　pages cm
　　Includes bibliographical references.
　　LCCN 2015944691
　　ISBN 978-1-60414-872-5 (paperback)

　　1. Yale University—History. 2. Yale University—Corrupt practices. 3. Universities and colleges—Business management. 4. College costs. I. Title. II. Title: Yale and the Ivy League cartel.

LD6334.R63 2015　　　　　　378.746'8
　　　　　　　　　　　　　　QBI15-600144

(Provided by Quality Books, Inc.)

First Edition
First Printing July 2015
Printed in the United States of America
10 9 8 7 6 5 4 3 2 1

Fideli Publishing Inc. • 119 W. Morgan St. • Martinsville, IN 46151 • **888-343-3542**

www.FideliPublishing.com

Note of Appreciation

Herman J. Lippke and William Brinkerhoff Jackson provided the money that made possible my college education at Old Yale. I am very grateful to them. — ESR

Contents

Preface

This book describes the Ivy League Cartel that prevents tuition-price competition and explains how the illegal cartel has been preserved by skillful lawyering and political support of the academic establishment. The book traces the development of one member of the cartel (Yale) from a college with a purpose to an institution with no purpose other than maximization of revenue.

I watched this happen. I graduated from Yale College in 1948 as a scholarship student – the same year as George H. W. Bush and about 1000 other young men, and three years later from Yale Law School.

Before applying for admission I had never seen Yale. No one in my family had been to Yale. I had never met a Yale graduate. Bush's father graduated from Yale. My father spent a year at Lafayette. Bush graduated from Andover. I graduated from a co-educational Quaker boarding school from which, so far as I know, no one before me had ever gone to Yale.

Public schools in Pennsylvania taught me to read and write English, as well as a little Latin and some French, and how to do arithmetic. We were also given courses in mechanical drawing, woodwork, cutting and soldering metal, and electrical wiring. This was before the education establishment had adopted the assumptions that you can teach anybody anything and that it is unfair to prepare some young people for a life of working with their hands.

I had no difficulty competing with Andover graduates in class work at Yale. Academically, George Bush was no better prepared than I was. Socially, I was never in his league, or even in the game. Extra-curricular activities were a large component of an Old Yale education.

My first six school years were in central Pennsylvania farm country near Harrisburg, the first five years in a one-story building named for Herbert Hoover with central heating and indoor plumbing but not much else. Each room contained two grades and one teacher who taught all subjects.

When I was in sixth grade my family moved to an area served by a one-room school with a privy out back and a kerosene stove in the rear of the room. Twenty-seven children of various ages from six to sixteen required by law to attend sat in rows facing the teacher with a slate blackboard behind him. Divided into grades one through eight, we were taught by one man how to sit still, and how to read, write and do arithmetic. Disorderly conduct resulted in being required, during recess and lunch periods, to write on the blackboard 100 times: "If I don't mend my ways, I will end up in jail." Corporal punishment was sometimes employed.

The school year ran from the end of the harvest season in the Fall to the beginning of planting season in the Spring, so that children were available to work on farms. Everyone except the teacher walked to school, regardless of the distance or the weather. There were no holidays except Christmas.

From seventh through tenth grades I attended public schools in suburban Philadelphia for which my one-room school had prepared me adequately in every respect. For my last two years of high school I was sent to George School in Bucks County, near Trenton, New Jersey. Prior to visiting Yale to seek a scholarship, I had never been farther south than Washington, DC, (to which my grandmother took me and my cousins as boys to see the monuments), or farther north than New York City, (to which my father took me to see the Statue of Liberty).

When I entered Yale, I was well prepared academically. I obtained uniformly good marks. My freshman courses, as I recall, were: a survey of English literature that included Chaucer, Shakespeare and Brooks and Warren's "Understanding Poetry"; a course in 18th century French literature conducted in French, (Moliere, Racine, Pascal); Physics; and a differential calculus course in which I received a mark of "100" on the final exam, having solved all the problems correctly, the result not of great intellect but of early academic discipline.

Andover graduates like George Bush knew what they were doing at Yale in a way that I never did. I was there to get a college diploma so that I could go to law school. It was many years after graduation and much reflection before I began to understand what Yale was all about. Bush was following a family tradition. His father was an alumnus of distinction. My father dropped out of Lafayette College after one year, uncomfortable with the financial strain on his divorced mother.

My father inherited a name that suggests substantial inherited wealth, but he did not inherit any money to go with it, and he thought life was too short to spend it building net worth. We were never hungry while I was growing up, but there was no loose cash around. Chicken at Grandmother's on Sunday was a treat. If I were to go to Yale, it was not obvious where the money was coming from to send me there.

The money came from, among others, Herman J. Lippke and William Brinkerhoff Jackson, people whom I have never met and about whom I know nothing. They paid my tuition through what were called "scholarships" for students with superior records.

My family never paid anything for me to go through Yale except for second-hand books, train fares when I didn't hitch-hike, and discounted room bills. I earned my meals by working in a print shop, as a file clerk in the dean's office and as a library assistant. Cash for beer and tickets to football games came from unloading freight cars, raking leaves, ushering at concerts and baby-sitting for faculty members.

YALE

&

THE IVY LEAGUE CARTEL

How a college lost its soul and became a hedge fund

CHAPTER I

What is Yale?

Tthere is much indiscriminate use of the word "Yale." There is Yale College and Yale University. There is Yale-New Haven Hospital, a travel agency named Yale Educational Travel and Yale-NUS in Singapore.

In answer to the question: what is Yale?, the editor of the alumni magazine has replied: "Yale evolved, from a college for prep school-educated Easterners to an international research university." The current president says, "Large numbers of applicants who deserve a Yale experience aren't admitted." When these people use the word "Yale," implying an identity and continuity, what are they talking about?

YALE IS A VALUABLE BRAND NAME

To make sense of the matter, "Yale" is best understood as a valuable trademark, a brand name attached to a variety of products, including college diplomas. The word adds value because of its association in the public mind with wealth, power and membership in a selective elite.

This brand was built over a period of 250 years by Old Yale. The people who now own the brand are quite different from those who created it. The owners of Old Yale shared a purpose — Education of Suitable Youth. That Yale is dead, but the brand remains very much alive.

Anthony Kronman has written in the *Yale Alumni Magazine:*

> "Even a half-century ago, the question of life's meaning had a more central and respected place in higher education than it does today. Institutions of higher learning felt they had the right and duty to address …the question of how to spend one's life, of what to care about and why, of which relations, projects and pleasures are capable of giving life purpose and value."

There is no consensus among the current owners of the Yale brand what education consists of or of which youth might be suitable to receive it. Addressing the incoming Yale College class in September 2007, the president of Yale University said:

> "It is true that your professors are unlikely to give you the answers to questions about what you should value and how you should live. We leave that up to you."

The owners of today's Yale brand have no shared purpose other than maximization of revenues. What began as a college, an educational institution, has become, in the words of the alumni magazine editor, "radically different in population and priorities from what it used to be." It is now a commercial enterprise marketing a

The ARMS of Yale University

THE coat of arms of Yale University is blazoned: *azure* (blue); upon an open book, edges gold (or yellow), covers and ties silver (or white) the letters אורים ותמים *sable* (black). The motto LUX ET VERITAS is usually inscribed beneath the shield on a ribbon.

The Yale arms may be displayed in full color or in black and white; they may be surrounded by ivy, laurel or elm leaves. They may be drawn within any proper ornamental border or cartouche but without helmet, crest, mantling, or supporters. They form the distinctive decoration used by Yale men and Yale associations.

The source of the arms is the device upon the seal adopted by the Trustees of Yale College in the early eighteenth century. The unknown designer identified the Book as the Bible by characters which read "Urim and Thummim," probably names of sacred lots to be cast for the purpose of ascertaining the divine will (cf. Exodus 28:30; I Samuel 14:40 f.; Ezra 2:63). Their suggestion that the Book contains divine revelations would be clear to scholars who read the Scriptures in the original Hebrew. But for others the designer added a translation in the vernacular.

When the translation of the Old Testament was made in Greek, the real meaning of "Urim and Thummim" was no longer known and different words were used in different passages to translate them. Among the renderings given were "Light" and "Truth," and it is this interpretation which was chosen for the seal-legend and placed outside of the shield in Latin: Lux et Veritas.

The seal bears the arms within the circular inscription—Sigill:Coll:Yalen:Nov:Port:Nov: Angl. It is the property of the President and Fellows of the University and the symbol of their legal authority. The seal is impressed upon official documents of the University for the purpose of authenticating signatures and should be used in no other way.

3

valuable brand on coffee mugs, sweatshirts, river cruises and diplomas in Latin that few can read.

WHAT IS A CARTEL?

A cartel is a combination of independent commercial enterprises designed to limit competition. In 1890 Congress made participation in such organizations a federal crime, punishable by fines and imprisonment. Today's Yale, the institution to which the magazine editor and president refer when they use the term, is a commercial enterprise that belongs to a cartel.

YALE COLLEGE HAS NOT JUST CHANGED; IT NO LONGER EXISTS

One-room schools no longer exist in Pennsylvania, nor does the Yale College from which George Bush and I graduated in 1948. The buildings, the library and the name are still there, but the college with a purpose and high standards is not. A good education may still be available, but it is not required. A college created by Christian ministers, who believed that education had content and purpose, is now run by financial manipulators, indifferent to what is taught.

In 1948, the college was not yet so thoroughly dependent on government, not yet regarded as a global quasi-public utility. There was still something special, something distinctive, about Yale, what Brooks Mather Kelley called "a soul ... uniquely hers." Something of that soul was expressed in music.

Glee clubs of each graduating class were organized in the late 1860s. The University Glee Club was organized at about the same time. Members of the classes of 1909 and 1910 brought together the Whiffenpoofs.

Brian Hooker, 1902 wrote the following verse to which Seth Bingham, 1904 wrote the music:

"Mother of Men, grown strong in giving

Honor to them thy lights have led;

Rich in the toil of thousands living,

Proud of the deeds of thousands dead.

We who have felt thy pow'r and known thee,

We in whose work thy gifts avail,

High in our hearts, enshrined, enthrone thee,

Mother of Men, Old Yale.

Spirit of Youth, alive, unchanging,

Under whose feet the years are cast,

Heir to an ageless empire, ranging

Over the future and the past;

Thee, whom our fathers loved before us,

Thee, whom our sons unborn shall hail,

Praise we today in sturdy chorus,

Mother of Men, Old Yale."

One element of the soul of Old Yale was a gentleman's healthy but respectful interest in women. That soul is dead — replaced by Sex Week. The "Yale Man" no longer exists.

TODAY'S YALE IS SEX WITHOUT RESTRAINT

Nathan Harden in his book *Sex and God at Yale* (2012), writes that today's Yale "has publicly welcomed the most extreme elements of the sex industry onto the campus" and has "moved beyond simply being permissive, to actively promoting a low-minded sexual agenda."

In 2011, Undergraduates for a Better Yale College petitioned the university to withdraw its support of Sex Week at Yale, deploring what it called "Yale's prevailing hook-up culture," where "freshman are pressured to accept inebriated hook-ups as the default lifestyle."

The principal distinction of today's Yale may be its reputation as "the Gay Ivy." The July 2009 issue of the *Yale Alumni Magazine* celebrated the fact that "Yale has been widely known as the Gay Ivy since at least 1987. ... Yale probably ... [has] a higher proportion of gay students than other Ivies; there are no statistics, but many gay Yale students think it's true. ... Yale is a gay-friendly school. The campus is unusually welcoming to gay and lesbian students and has an active, multifaceted gay social scene."

SCHOLARSHIPS HAVE BEEN REPLACED BY
SECRET DISCRIMINATORY DISCOUNTS

Scholarships of the sort I earned, made possible by generous alumni, have been eliminated by agreement among members of the Ivy League. A system of secret discriminatory discounting, called "financial aid" making it sound charitable, and so-called "need-blind admission" has been developed. The system avoids any pressure to lower tuitions and makes possible tuition increases without discouraging applications for admission, so that an impressive ratio of rejections to admissions is maintained. This maximizes revenue and preserves a reputation for exclusivity, on which much of the luster of today's Yale depends.

CHAPTER II

Seven Christian Ministers & a Rich Man

OLD YALE HAD A MISSION

On November 11, 1701, with the permission and financial support of the colonial legislature of Connecticut, seven Christian ministers — Samuel Andrew, Thomas Buckingham, Israel Chauncy, James Pierpont, Abraham Pierson, Noadiah Russell and Joseph Webb — met in Saybrook, Connecticut, to establish a college. In the founding document, the clergymen affirmed their intention to continue the purpose of their fathers in coming to America — to plant and propagate "the blessed Reformed, Protestant Religion" and to do this by "Liberal and Relligious (sic) Education of Suitable Youth." The college was to be known as the Collegiate School and to teach "the Liberal Arts, and Languages." There were nine students in the graduating class of 1714, the largest to that date.

In September 1717, trustees of the college who favored a move from Saybrook to New Haven purchased an acre and a half facing the New Haven Green at what is now the corner of Chapel and College Streets occupied by Bingham Hall. The school began with books brought to Connecticut by the first settlers. In 1714, Jeremiah Dummer, Connecticut's agent in England, sent the school more than 800 additional volumes. These included works of Boyle, Locke, Newton, Halley, Raleigh, Steele, Chaucer, Milton and Bacon.

In October 1717, building began in New Haven. Courted by Dummer in England, Elihu Yale gave to the college books, a portrait of King George I, and goods that the college sold in Boston. As a result, Mr. Yale's name went on the building. Yale had made a fortune with the East India Company as governor of Madras. His grandmother, father and uncle had helped to settle New Haven. His father, David Yale, once owned the land on which Jonathan Edwards College was built in 1932.

There is some uncertainty in the historical documents as to just when the Collegiate School became Yale College, but, with Yale's name on the school's only building, it was not long before the institution became known as Yale. The second major structure, a brick building, was completed in 1753 and named Connecticut Hall, having been built with money provided by the colonial legislature.

In 1743, the president taught all the courses, assisted by two tutors. The curriculum described by the president in his introduction to the library catalog, included Languages, Arithmetic and Algebra in the first year: Logic, Rhetoric and Geometry in the second year; Mathematics and Natural Philosophy in the third year; and Ethics and Divinity in the fourth year. In 1745, a third tutor was added, allowing a tutor for each of the lower classes. The president taught the seniors.

OLD YALE HAD A HERO

Nathan Hale was granted a B.A. degree from Yale College in 1773. Serving as intelligence officer in George Washington's army, he was caught by the British and hung as a spy at 11 am on September 22, 1776, on a tree in the Dove Tavern Artillery Park at what is now on Third Avenue between 66th and 68th Streets on the Upper East Side of Manhattan, according to *The Memorial Quadrangle — a Book about Yale* com-piled by Robert Dudley French, (New Haven 1929). Hale is reported to have said, "I only regret that I have but one life to lose for my country."

In 1775 there were about 900 living graduates of Yale College. One third of them were Christian ministers. One graduate in five fought against the British. Nine percent of them died in the war. In 1781, total enrollment in the college was 224. In 1817, Yale was the largest college in the country, and had a library of 7,000 volumes.

Yale granted its first medical degree in 1814. In 1823, the religious oath that had been required of all presidents, fellows, professors and tutors was dropped. A school of engineering was established in 1852, a scientific school in 1854, an art school in 1866 and a music school in 1890. Yale was the first major institution of higher education to have an art school. Yale Law School, begun as a separate institution in 1800, first granted Yale degrees to two students in 1843.

In 1865 there were more than four thousand living graduates of Yale. Twenty-five served as generals in the Union Army; six, as generals in the Army of the Confederacy. The Yale Daily News was founded in 1878. It claims to be the oldest college daily.

H.S.Durand, a Yale College graduate in the class of 1881, wrote the following words to be sung to the music of "Die Wacht am Rhein:"

Bright College years, with pleasure rife,
The shortest, gladdest years of life;
How swiftly are ye gliding by!
Oh, why doth time so quickly fly?
The seasons come, the seasons go,
The earth is green or white with snow,
But time and change shall naught avail
To break the friendships formed at Yale.

We all must leave this college home,
About the stormy world to roam;
But though the mighty ocean's tide
Should us from dear old Yale divide,
As round the oak the ivy twines
The clinging tendrils of its vines,
So are our hearts close bound to Yale
By ties of love that ne'er shall fail.

2

Bright College Years

H. S. Durand, '81

Carl Wilhelm
Edited and arranged by
Marshall Bartholomew

86143

In after years, should troubles rise
To cloud the blue of sunny skies,
How bright will seem, through mem'ry's haze
Those happy, golden, bygone days!
Oh, let us strive that ever we
May let these words our watch-cry be,
Where'er upon life's sea we sail:
"For God, for Country and for Yale!"

OLD YALE HAD A HISTORY OF WHICH IT WAS PROUD

Today's Yale is ignorant of, or ashamed of its history. Admission policy aimed at preserving Old Yale as a predominately Christian institution is now viewed as crude and ignorant anti-Semitism, accepting that portrayal by a professor of psychology at UC Berkeley in his book *The Chosen*. God and Country have been replaced by Diversity and Globalism.

A statue of Nathan Hale still stands outside Connecticut Hall, but his place as foremost Yale hero can be said to have been taken by David Swenson, manager of investments. The current president has a Yale Ph. D. in psychology. He, his immediate predecessor, and Swenson all went to college at Stanford.

The liberal arts college, founded by Christian ministers with a sense of purpose who believed that education had content, has been swallowed up and eclipsed by an international university directed more toward research than to teaching, managed by financiers with no overriding purpose other than to maximize secret financial holdings.

CHAPTER III

Old Yale, Mother of Men

Old Yale was not a younger brother trying to catch up to an older brother John Harvard. Yale was different. The difference was not just in location or comparative youth. An element of distinctiveness was the importance of competitive extra-curricular activities in Yale college life. In his message to the Yale Banner for 1948, President Charles Seymour stated his commitment to "maintaining the healthy balance between studies and extra-curricular activity which has always characterized Yale."

SKULL & BONES SILENTLY DOMINATED
UNDERGRADUATE LIFE

A club of undergraduates, to which Harvard had nothing comparable, played a dominant role. Phi Beta Kappa was the first secret society at Yale, founded in 1780. In the early 1800s, as a result of national sentiment against secret organizations, the chapter was closed. Within a few years a new club with no outside affiliation took its place. The club had the name "Skull & Bones." Classmates Alphonso Taft and William Russell founded the club in 1832. Taft's son, William Howard Taft, who went on to become President of

Skull & Bones

the United States as well as Chief Justice, joined the club while at Yale.

The club still exists but no longer has the importance it once did. The clubhouse is an imposing brownstone building on High Street just across the street from the Old Campus. It was built in three stages, in 1856, 1903, and 1911. Set back from the street, it looks like a giant tomb, a silent but bold statement of the message: "Keep Out."

From 1886 to 1921, every president of Yale had been a member. President Porter, who was president from 1871 to 1886 graduated from the college in 1831, a year before the club was established. (James Rowland Angell, president from 1921 to 1937, was not an alumnus of Yale College.)

Charles Seymour, president from 1937 to 1951, was the last president who belonged. Before becoming president he had been a distinguished scholar of history.

His retirement might be seen as the beginning of the end of Old Yale. His successor, Whitney Griswold, known primarily for his wit and not much else, was

Charles Seymour

commonly called "Whit." He was not a member of Skull & Bones. As an undergraduate, Griswold had gone with his friend Paul Mellon into Wolf's Head, an imitator of Skull & Bones that had a reputation for social and financial prominence.

For many years, fifteen seniors selected at the end of their junior year by their predecessors met every Thursday night in a building with no windows to which non-members were never admitted. What went on inside the building was kept secret, leading to speculation about bizarre initiation rites.

Unlike the Seven Society at the University of Virginia, whose members' identity is first revealed publicly only in their obituaries, or Phi at Princeton, its existence and membership were widely advertised. In the early 1920s names of those invited to join were published on the front page of *The New York Times*. The club with the attention-getting name maintained a balance of secrecy and notoriety.

17

Other "secret societies" have been established at today's Yale. The 1948 *Yale Banner,* the student yearbook, contained a section on "Honors" immediately following the class officers. The section began with photographs of the buildings of six societies in order of their establishment from 1832 to 1903 with lists of their members — Skull & Bones and five others that served as consolation prizes for the strivers who did not make it and dinner clubs for the well-to-do, more exclusive than the dining halls of the "junior fraternities" like Delta Kappa Epsilon, Zeta Psi and the Fence Club.

In 1948, when George H. W. Bush graduated from Yale College, the conspicuous windowless buildings of the secret societies in the center of the campus to which approximately one undergraduate in ten belonged provided daily reminders of the primacy of Skull & Bones, the apex of success in Yale undergraduate life.

According to the *Yale Alumni Magazine,* "there are now at least 44 societies ... most of them [with] around 15 members, meaning that nearly half the seniors now belong to one society or another."

Old Yale was competitive. Members of Skull & Bones were certified winners. God and Country were part of the soul of Old Yale. Skull & Bones was its backbone. The power and influence over world affairs of this small club of college students has often been overestimated by journalists, but its role inside the college was central.

Membership in Skull & Bones was unique certification that the member was a success at Yale, unlike Phi Beta Kappa, which returned to New Haven after a period of banishment, but has remained only barely visible.

People who know little about Yale were over-impressed when it was discovered that the nominees for president of the United

States of both major political parties, John Kerry and George H. W. Bush, were members of Skull & Bones.

The secrecy of the clubhouse and the list of members who have distinguished themselves in public life make sensational newspaper copy. An alumna of the current Yale published a book several years ago about the club, complete with floor plans of the clubhouse and the results of interviews of more than a hundred of its members, disclosing every secret she could uncover through years of effort. As an undergraduate she had been a member of the oldest of the club's imitators with its own windowless building. She said she had joined "for the free liquor."

It should not be surprising that, among fifteen young men, selected annually from hundreds of college students, who themselves had come through a selective process for admission and three years of survival in a competitive environment, there would be some who would later play prominent roles in public life. If one looks at the numbers over a century, it is remarkable, not that there have been so many, but that there have been so few who reached national prominence. For many members, the invitation to join was the high point in their lives from which they went on to prosperous middle class obscurity. Membership was a valued mark of distinction, not participation in a sinister conspiracy intent on power.

The Skull & Bones to which generations of Bushes and John Kerry belonged was an exclusive supper club of competitive winners, a small group of seniors who had succeeded at Old Yale, and nothing more.

CHAPTER IV

William F. Buckley, Jr.

Charles Seymour, the last president of Yale University who was a member of Skull & Bones, graduated from Yale College in 1908. He joined the faculty as a professor of history and was Yale's president from 1937 to 1951. He valued the character, traditions and soul of Old Yale.

In the Fall of 1949, the Dean of Freshmen instructed staff of the Freshman Dining Hall to refuse admission to any freshman not wearing a coat and tie. An editorial in the *Yale Daily News* applauded this policy and expressed support for efforts of residential col-lege masters to require the wearing of a tie to dinner in the college din-ing halls, characterizing such action as demanding that members of the college show "evidence of the basic courtesies." At that time both the administration and the student body, although they never said so, placed a value on personal conduct — and felt that standards of appearance,

William F. Buckley Jr.

manner of speech and civility toward others were an important part of a Yale education.

Selected graduate students were hired to live on the Old Campus as models. They were called "Freshman Counselors" and assigned eighteen counselees, without any specification of what counsel they were expected to provide.

Freshmen lived on the old campus. Upperclassmen lived in the residential colleges. Each college had a master, a gentleman of some dignity and distinction. Sophomores were invited by the wives of residential college masters to Sunday afternoon tea at which sherry was served in proper glasses. There were no lectures or exams on the subject, but Old Yale, characterized derisively by some as a "manners school," taught boys how to talk, dress and act like gentlemen.

That Yale no longer exists. In December 1998 the master of Saybrook College, awaiting trial on a Federal charge of possessing child pornography, was reported by *The New York Times* to have been charged with sexually assaulting a 13-year-old boy. His collection of child pornography kept on two computers had been seized by the FBI at his office in Saybrook College.

At the same time that efforts were being made to preserve the atmosphere of Old Yale, nothing was done to include respect for traditional values of any kind in the curriculum. The editor of the *Yale Daily News,* William Frank Buckley, Jr., discovered what was obvious to anyone looking — that Yale College courses were encouraging students to look favorably on collectivism and unfavorably on religion.

Upon graduation and acceptance at both the graduate school and the law school, Buckley enrolled at neither but spent the next year collecting data documenting and writing about his discovery.

Facing Child Pornography Trial, Yale Professor Charged in Abuse

By MIKE ALLEN

NEW HAVEN, Dec. 22 — A Yale University professor awaiting trial on a Federal charge of possessing child pornography was charged Monday with sexually assaulting a 13-year-old boy.

The professor, Antonio Lasaga, was charged with two counts of first-degree sexual assault, risking injury to a minor and "promoting a minor in an obscene performance." The New Haven police, who would not provide details of the charges, arrested Mr. Lasaga at his home in Cheshire, Conn., where he was confined after officials determined he had violated the conditions of his release on the Federal charges. Bond was set at $250,000.

Mr. Lasaga had held the position of Master, a social adviser and mentor, at Saybrook College, one of the residential colleges where Yale undergraduates sleep and eat.

He resigned from his duties there in November after agents of the Federal Bureau of Investigation seized two computers from his office at the college.

Two weeks after the raid on Mr. Lasaga's office, he was charged with the receipt and possession of child pornography. A statement by the United States Attorney's office in New Haven asserted that Mr. Lasaga had "downloaded from the Internet, and kept numerous images of, child pornography."

He was released on the condition that he have no contact with minor children until his case was resolved.

But on Dec. 9, he was placed on home confinement with electronic monitoring after Federal prosecutors asserted that he had been seen

Stephen J. Boitano/The New Haven Register

Antonio Lasaga is a professor of geochemistry at Yale University.

driving back and forth in front of the home of a child and "was observed parked at the minor child's bus stop shortly before the bus was due to arrive."

A Yale official said Mr. Lasaga remains on paid leave from his position as a professor of geochemistry.

Thomas P. Conroy, Yale's acting director of public affairs, issued a statement calling the new charges "very serious and deeply troubling."

"The university will continue to follow the developments very closely," the statement said. "As more facts become available, the university will make a decision about what to do next."

23

NEW BLOOD COMES IN FROM THE MIDWEST

In 1947 Yale College's traditional course in local government about mayors, corruption and reform had been replaced with a course titled "Politics and the Modern Local Community" taught by a new member of the faculty, Willmoore Kendall, who was taken on that year as an Associate Professor.

Kendall was an excellent teacher, courteous and patient with students. Accessible and friendly, a master of the Socratic method, he was a man of great personal charm. His course for undergraduates was deceptively named. The course contained little about municipal government but was an introduction to political theory. Kendall introduced his students to concepts, ideas and questions about government that stayed with them for the rest of their lives. He taught students how to think about politics.

Buckley took the course. In a letter published in *YAM*, March/April 2012 at p.6, an alumnus describes what happened as follows:

> "As an intensive major in government, I was required to take a year-long junior seminar in political theory, taught then by Professor Willmoore Kendall, the conservative political science professor. Imagine my surprise when I showed up for the opening meeting of the seminar in September 1950, to find that I had been joined by six seniors, led by Bill Buckley and Brent Bozell.
>
> "We met weekly in Kendall's living room. Much of the class took place about three feet above my brain. What I remember about the class itself is that I was privileged to attend a weekly animated

Willmoore Kendall

discussion in which Kendall consistently, and forcefully, took Buckley's reasoning down. Perhaps the course should have been titled 'The Education of William Buckley'."

The head of the government department at that time was a young professor of no particular distinction. The most popular professor in the department was a man approaching retirement. He read polished lectures with a trace of a British accent to large halls in which every seat was taken. The lectures were carefully prepared and impressively delivered. Students listened attentively for fifty minutes and left with a feeling that they had imbibed great profundities. Ten minutes later they could recall little of what had been said.

Kendall's attitude toward faculty colleagues ranged from indifference to contempt. He regarded the popular lecturer as an "historian," a member of the "do-nothing school of political science." The others he saw as incompetent. As he said, they did not "know the literature." Kendall knew the literature.

Kendall was from Oklahoma, the son of a Methodist minister who was blind. The boy learned to read at an early age and was used by his father as a reader. By the time he was twelve he had read most of classical literature. He graduated from high school at thirteen and from the University of Oklahoma at eighteen. He attended Oxford as a Rhodes Scholar. He went to Spain during the Spanish Civil War. He received a Ph. D. in political science from the University of Illinois in 1940. His thesis, *John Locke and the Doctrine of Majority Rule*, remains a classic of political science literature.

While Buckley was the chief editor of the *Yale Daily News*, Kendall wrote letters to the *News*. Buckley published them. Their flavor is indicated by the following paragraph from a letter published in the *Yale Daily News* of April 28, 1950:

> "I am an old-fashioned majority-rule democrat; i.e. I believe it to be not only the right but the *duty* of the people of a democratic nation to use public policy as an instrument for creating the kind of society their values call for, and, to that end, to make public policy in accordance with their own lights. I regard any attempt to place certain matters (e.g. freedom of speech, freedom of the press, etc.) beyond their reach, via enshrinement in a bill of rights regarded as not subject to modification (with or without a Supreme Court to act as its guardian) as *ipso facto* undemocratic. And the reason I believe such attempts to be undemocratic is, quite simply, that their demonstrable purpose is to substitute someone else's values and lights for those of the people — for which, at the margin, we must of course be prepared to read 'the majority of the people.'"

Buckley and Kendall spent much time together. Kendall visited frequently as a houseguest at the Buckley family home in Sharon, Connecticut. Although probably one of the most sophisticated students of politics in the world, Kendall was not, himself, a politician. He did not tailor what he said to please those who might be listening. Kendall's main interest in life was political theory, especially the ideas of Locke and Rousseau, and in what he called "making sense." Buckley's main interest in life was Buckley and how to attract attention to himself. Buckley soaked up ideas from Kendall and lived on them as a celebrated public intellectual for the rest of his life.

In the fall of 1950 there was an election in Connecticut to fill a vacant seat in the US Senate. William Benton was the candidate of the Democrats. He had been appointed by his former partner in the advertising business, Chester Bowles, to fill Bowles' un-expired term when Bowles resigned, having been elected governor. Prescott Bush, father of George H. W. Bush, was the Republican candidate. The candidates made a joint appearance in the Yale Law School auditorium, a large paneled room with seats in theatre style and a balcony.

WILLIAM F. BUCKLEY, JR. MAKES HIS ENTRANCE ON THE PUBLIC SCENE

Two entrance doors in the rear of the auditorium opened to aisles down a sloping floor to a massive podium. Attendance was open to the public. Every seat was filled. Each candidate made a statement. Then the audience was invited to ask questions. The moment this opportunity came, a tall, self-assured young man, graduate of an army officer candidate school, more mature in appearance than the average undergraduate, got up from his seat in the back of the room, stepped into an aisle, took a few steps down toward the podium and assumed possession of the room.

In a loud clear voice he said, "My question is addressed to Senator Benton. You told us tonight that ... [here he alluded to something Benton had said] ...and you told us ... [alluding to another of Benton's statements] ... and you told us ... [alluding to a third]. Now my question is: … (substantial pause) … How many other LIES have you told us tonight?"

William F. Buckley, Jr. had made his entrance on the public stage.

As a senior at Yale, Buckley saw the inconsistency between the values held generally by Yale College alumni (Christianity and capitalism) and those that had greater appeal to much of the faculty (atheism or agnosticism and collectivism). He saw this as an opportunity and he took it. In the Fall of 1951 he published *God & Man at Yale.* To his surprise, the book sold 23,000 copies.

Writing in the *Yale Alumni Magazine* in 2008, Gaddis Smith said the "heart" of the book was Buckley's assertion "that the duel between Christianity and atheism is the most important in the world [and] … that the struggle between individualism and collectivism is the same struggle reproduced on another level." Smith is probably right that this assertion was the "heart" of the book. It is not clear that the assertion was Buckley's.

The published book attributed sole authorship to Buckley with no acknowledgement of assistance from Kendall, but, in the introduction to an edition published in 1977, Buckley said that these particular words "were not originally my own" but had been written by Kendall.

Buckley's response to the reception that this assertion provoked when the book was first published was one of delight at the attention it received. In 1977, he wrote:

> "When I saw the suggested formulation, written out on the margin of my manuscript in Willmoore Kendall's bold green script, I suspected

they (sic) would cause difficulty. But there was a nice rhetorical resonance and an intrinsic, almost nonchalant suggestion of an exciting symbiosis, so I let it pass."

One might wonder what Buckley was thinking about the assertion when he let it "pass" in 1951 or in 1977. Did he agree with the idea or disagree with it? Was this "heart of the book" only a matter of rhetorical "resonance and nonchalance"? He provided the following foggy answer to those questions:

"The words 'the same struggle reproduced on another level' were not originally my own. In the prolonged defense of the book I did not renounce them, in part out of loyalty to my mentor, in part, no doubt, because it would have proved embarrassing to disavow a formulation published over one's signature, never mind its provenance. But in part also because I was tickled by the audacity of the sally and not un-amused by the sputtering outrage of its critics."

As Buckley saw it, the "proposed formulation" written on the margin of his book draft presented "an opportunity to be audacious." Whether the assertion, which Gaddis says was the heart of the book, was valid or not was not important to him.

In an article published in the same *Yale Alumni Magazine* as that in which Smith's article appeared, Sam Tanenhaus wrote without indicating how he knew, that, "by mid-January [of 1951 Buckley] had completed enough of the manuscript to show it to Willmoore

Kendall, who covered the pages in green ink, honing its assertions, polishing its sentences, and deftly shaping what would become the book's most celebrated formulation." With Tanenhaus, the "formulation" was not just the "heart" of the book but "celebrated."

In 1971, Buckley acknowledged that he had had "help" from Kendall with the book. In the original publication there were no acknowledgements of any kind.

Kendall had a lifetime contract to join the Yale faculty as an Associate Professor. He was never promoted. After 14 years he accepted a cash settlement to leave. Had the institution valued diversity of views and been truly concerned about preserving "academic freedom," Kendall would have been promoted and urged to stay rather than eased out.

His departure ended the possibility of any reversal of the tide toward hospitality to atheism and socialism in New Haven and, with it, any hope for preservation of Old Yale. Kendall died in 1967 in Texas, where he was teaching at the University of Dallas. There was little public notice.

Although 16 years older than Buckley the college student, Kendall the college professor, a minister's son and country boy from Oklahoma, did not understand Buckley. Kendall failed to recognize Buckley's capacity to use and discard people in his efforts to attract attention and obtain establishment approval, a skill described in detail by Richard Brookhiser in *Right Time, Right Place* (Basic Books, 2009).

Kendall said one time that Buckley was the best friend he had ever had. He later learned painfully otherwise.

Evan Galbraith was a life-long close friend of Buckley's. They were club-mates in Skull & Bones. Galbraith was married to a woman who had insisted, against the advice of her father who was a pediatrician, on taking to term a pregnancy during which she had measles. The result was a severely handicapped daughter and a mentally unstable mother.

Mrs. Galbraith was infatuated with Willmoore Kendall. On a visit to Paris with her husband, she refused to return home with him and threw herself at Kendall. The approach was not welcomed by Kendall, who was accompanied at the time by his "secretary" and did not regard Mrs. Galbraith as physically attractive in any case.

When Galbraith proposed a divorce, his wife refused. Galbraith then sued her, naming Kendall as co-respondent based on Galbraith's assertion that his wife had claimed she had had an affair with Kendall in Paris. Buckley was in a unique position to help Kendall extricate himself from this embarrassment, but, when Kendall attempted to reach Buckley by phone for help to sort things out before they became public, Buckley could not be reached. The matter was eventually settled out of court.

In addition to his misapprehension of the nature of Buckley's friendship, Kendall also misunderstood the shallowness of Buckley's interest in ideas. Buckley was not interested in ideas the way Kendall was. Kendall was interested in ideas for their intrinsic value and intellectual challenge. Buckley was interested in ideas as vehicles for achieving personal notoriety.

Kendall once said that Buckley was "ruined by his first favorable mention in *Time Magazine*." Buckley was not ruined by favorable publicity. Buckley was made by favorable publicity. Personal attention had been his goal from the time of his brash performance in the Yale Law School auditorium.

Buckley had made clear in his first book that he was not trying to advocate anything but merely seeking to confront Yale alumni with the fact that their alma mater was not teaching young people to respect what they valued. As he wrote: "I cannot repeat too often that I have cause to object to current Yale policies only if there exists a disparity between the values the alumni *want* taught, and those currently *being* taught ..."

Buckley made no statement as to what values he thought should be taught, having no clear idea what they were. Buckley's cause as a young rebel was anti-communism. He knew what he was against, but he never thought through to an articulation of what he was for. He was happy with the label "conservative" without a definition of what he meant by it.

In an essay on "Academic freedom" first published in 1971, four years after his death, Kendall described what happened as follows.

> "Buckley, you might say, had gone to Yale thinking it was the old-fashioned kind of university. ... He soon found out it wasn't — that what it was trying to do to him was undermine — yes, undermine — his, and other students' belief in the orthodoxy that had once ridden high at Yale. He found that this was being done under the slogan "Academic Freedom!" — with an exclamation point, of course. ... And he found this paradox, or rather pair of paradoxes. The administrators of Yale, the President, the important deans, were all men who themselves still appeared to believe in the orthodoxy their university was undermin-

ing — paradox one. And the money for running Yale not only had come in the past but was still coming from men who believed in the orthodoxy. They were still in a position to say, "No more of this, or we give no more money, and where'll your university be then?" They were still in position to, yet didn't. Paradox two. So Buckley wrote *God and Man at Yale* to demand that Yale's alumni bring her to heel. And Yale, the Yale faculty, met Buckley head on. Running the university, deciding what kind of university it should be, was, it said, the faculty's business, not the alumni's. What Yale was doing — what, concretely, it was doing about the old orthodoxies, was — well, exactly what it should be doing, and certainly what it was going to keep on doing. And overnight, Buckley got what I imagine to have been the surprise of his very surpriseful life. For the alumni, instead of rallying behind him, tacitly rallied behind the faculty. Instead of themselves becoming angry, at being told that Yale was none of their business, they tacitly accepted that view of the matter, and still kept on giving their money — soon, indeed, were giving their money more generously than ever. Buckley, at least on the battleground he had chosen, took a licking. Soon, indeed, Yale had a President who, unlike his predecessor, was the very embodiment of the new ideas on academic freedom, and Yale became, even more unabashedly, the kind of university Buckley had accused it of being."

Buckley became a celebrity as an iconoclast opposed to the trend of things. He wanted the approval of the establishment, worked hard for it, and eventually obtained it. In 1997, he was invited to join the Yale faculty to teach a course, not in government or politics, but in English composition, and three years later was given an honorary doctor's degree. The *Yale Alumni Magazine* devoted most of an entire issue to him. When he died,

Yale Alumni Magazine
Memorial Issue.

a memorial Mass was held at St. Patrick's Cathedral in New York City. Henry Kissinger gave a eulogy to some 2000 people. There is now a William F. Buckley Program at Yale, which brings speakers to campus.

Buckley made a career as a merchandiser of other peoples' ideas. He never developed a political philosophy of his own. He called himself a conservative but had no clear idea what he wanted to conserve or why. He was a journalist, not a political philosopher.

Richard Brookhiser, Buckley's acolyte for many years, in his book *Right Time, Right Place* says, "Bill was haunted off and on by an unwritten book, which would have applied Ortega y Gassett's *Revolt of the Masses* to mid-twentieth century America. Willmoore Kendall had urged the project on him, but it never got done." Jose Ortega y Gassett's 1930 book had been reissued in the United States in 1957.

John B. Judis in his 1988 book on Buckley says that Buckley tentatively selected a title *Revolt Against the Masses* and wrote about ten thousand words during two months he spent in Switzerland. According to Judis, Buckley "set aside his winter vacation in Switzerland for working on the book. He talked Hugh Kenner into accompanying him and Pat [his wife] to Saanen. ... Anxious to avoid solitary reflection, Buckley hoped that he would be inspired to write the book by daily discussions with Kenner."

The book never was written. Kenner later recalled that for Buckley "thought had become reflex." He was unable to resolve the philosophical contradictions in his own thinking. Paul Weiss, professor of philosophy at Yale, is said by Judis to have thought that Buckley "may have lacked the intellectual capacity for philosophical reflection."

THE VENTRILOQUIST AND THE DUMMY

There was a period during which anyone familiar with Kendall could watch Buckley's TV show *Firing Line,* close his eyes, and hear Kendall talking. Kendall was Edgar Bergen, the ventriloquist; Buckley was Charlie McCarthy, the dummy. Buckley's lips were moving, but Kendall was doing the talking. Kendall's writings remain thought-provoking and useful to anyone who wishes to think seriously about government. Buckley left nothing of lasting significance in all his books, newspaper columns, speeches, articles and TV shows. He was a comet, not a star.

Kendall and Buckley together might have made a contribution toward preserving Old Yale, but they did not. There was no effective opposition from the alumni to what was being taught or not taught at Yale in 1951. After the retirement of President Seymour, those in charge made no effort to preserve Old Yale, but hastened its demise. Buckley and Kendall might have slowed the dismantling and collapse, but preservation of Old Yale was not important to either of them.

CHAPTER V

Kingman Brewster, Jr.

Seymour's successor, Whitney Griswold '29, was a history professor of little distinction. He was President of Yale from 1950 to 1963, when he died in office. Following graduation from Yale College in 1929, he had gone to Wall Street, soon tired of it, returned to New Haven as a graduate student and never again left. He may have had some affection for Old Yale, but he did little to preserve it. Fearful that Buckley's book would adversely affect alumni contributions, Griswold tried to prevent its publication. Once the book was published, he rejected any possibility of exercising any influence over the content of education at Yale as violating "academic freedom."

Kingman Brewster, Jr. '41 was Provost of Yale University when Griswold died. After a lengthy search for an alternative, the Yale Corporation, by a divided vote, selected Brewster as President. He held the office until 1977, when he left to be US Ambassador in London. He did more than any other single individual to dismantle Old Yale.

BREWSTER HAD LITTLE AFFECTION FOR OLD YALE

As an undergraduate, Brewster had declined membership in Skull & Bones. He came from a highly educated family that included college presidents. He was a descendant of an important Mayflower passenger. He was sufficiently confident of his position in life that he did not need a seal of approval bestowed by college students, especially mid-westerners. After service in the Navy he went to Harvard Law School from which he graduated in 1948. From 1950 to 1960 he was on its faculty. In 1960 he moved back to New Haven as Provost of the University.

Buckley's book had made clear that the prevailing attitude of the Yale faculty was not one of reverence for either God or capitalism. Belief in omnipotent caring government replaced them both. Brewster kept the institution in the national tide of progressivism.

THE CHAPLAIN PLAYED A SUBSTANTIAL ROLE IN THE DISMANTLING OF OLD YALE

Brewster made William Coffin '49 chaplain of the university and said he was the best chaplain Yale had ever had. Coffin is reputed to have said he wasn't sure whether Kingman believed in God but he was sure that God believed in Kingman.

Endowed with musical aptitude, linguistic ability and unusual energy, Coffin wasted his talents on attention-getting and relentless self-promotional mischief ruining the lives of other people. As a young army officer in Germany at the end of World War II he was required to assist in forcibly shipping back to the Soviet Union refugees from Stalin's Russia. He became a courageous Cold Warrior, training naïve young volunteers how to jump out of airplanes into the Ukraine. Through no fault of his, they were all caught and promptly executed.

Coffin then became a Christian minister. He neglected his family and failed twice at marriage. He encouraged illegal draft resistance. When prosecuted and convicted for his illegal action, he weaseled out of his own responsibility, leaving young people to take the legal consequences for theirs. Seymour's Yale would have been ashamed of Coffin.

Through admissions policy Brewster made Yale less of a manners school. He is quoted as having said he did not want to be head of a boys' finishing school on Long Island Sound, indicating how he felt about Old Yale. In the 1960s, as out-of-wedlock sexual activity became socially acceptable, young men wanted easy access to women. Fearing a decline of applicants, Brewster explored possible mergers with women's colleges, including Vassar, but Vassar could not be persuaded to move to New Haven. Desperate that Yale might be left behind in attracting desirable applicants, Yale invited women to apply for admission. In September of 1969, the incoming freshman class was composed of approximately 50% women.

From Brewster on, Yale has been a follower, not a leader, a cork swept along by a national tide of abandonment of conformity to standards of manners and dress replaced by conformity to politically correct thought.

LITERACY NO LONGER A REQUIREMENT FOR ADMISSION

In 1998 the Yale College Class of 1948 published *We of '48, A Gathering Memoir of the Half Century.* Drawing on reports in the *Yale Alumni Magazine* at that time, I submitted the following description of what had become of Old Yale.

"Academic excellence is no longer a basic criterion for either admission or scholarships.

Important now is the 'strong hunch' as to whether the candidate has 'moral concern' or 'potential for leadership.' Children of alumni, athletes, and select 'minorities' receive preferential treatment. As one dean says, 'Perfect transcripts are perfectly compatible with utterly uninteresting minds.' Whether the admissions officer feels he would want to sit across from 'the applicant in the dining hall or share a bathroom with him' may be decisive.

"In 1968 Yale began teaching freshman prospects how to 'upgrade' their 'skills,' but 'many students' arrive with 'serious writing problems.' There are three 'beginning' English courses. Each residential college has writing (and mathematics) tutors. One tutor was 'shocked at the level of preparation' of some of those admitted. They 'didn't learn any grammar in school.'"

The '93-'94 course catalog offered 2,000 term courses with a major in Film Studies and language courses in Hausa, Yoruba, Kiswahili, and Zulu. Upon request, instruction has also been provided in Bamanekan, Fula, Igbo, Kikuyu, Kituba, Haitian Kreol, Shona, Twi, and West African Krio. Women's Studies 450b, Photography and Images of the Body, "examines" medical, documentary, and surveillance photographs, including works of Mapplethorpe.

The residential college system was undermined. In 1984 more than fifteen percent of the undergraduates lived off-campus. In 1995 undergraduates were allowed to use their meal cards to purchase $100 worth of food at local restaurants each semester. More than 1,000 signed up for the program.

ROTC was abolished. According to the *New York Times* in September 2012,

> "Amid the unrest stemming from the Vietnam War and subsequently from policies over gay soldiers, four of the eight Ivy League schools —— Harvard, Yale, Brown and Columbia — parted ways with campus ROTC.
>
> "Three Ivies — Harvard, Yale and Columbia — moved to bring ROTC back after the 2010 repeal of the Don't Ask Don't Tell policy for gays in the military. These promises are coming to fruition this fall. Yale University is holding a 'ribbon-cutting' on Sept. 21 to welcome back ROTC."

CHAPTER VI

Development of the Cartel

LACKING PURPOSE, BUT POSSESSED OF A VALUABLE BRAND NAME, THE NEW YALE JOINS A PRICE-FIXING CARTEL

Boat clubs from Yale and Harvard met on New Hampshire's Lake Winnipesauki in 1852 for what is said to be the first athletic competition between two U.S. colleges. In 1873 representatives of Columbia, Princeton, Rutgers and Yale met to establish rules for athletic contests between them. Harvard was invited but did not attend.

In 1945 the presidents of Brown, Columbia, Cornell, Dartmouth, Harvard, Penn, Princeton and Yale signed an Ivy Group Agreement. It provided:

> "The members of the Group reaffirm their prohibition of athletic scholarships. Athletes shall be admitted as students and awarded financial aid only on the basis of the same academic standards and economic need as are applied to all other students."
>
> In 1954 the Ivy Group Agreement was extended to all sports competition between schools in what has become known as the "Ivy League."

By agreeing to refrain from granting athletic scholarships or by lowering academic standards for superior athletes, these schools have prevented financial competition among themselves for athletes.

The result has been that their athletic teams are composed only of real college students and not semi-professional athletes. This has kept Yale from being competitive nationally in football, as it once was. The Yale Bowl, with 64,000 seats, is seldom filled.

A SPORTS LEAGUE BECAME A CARTEL DESIGNED TO AVOID PRICE COMPETITION FOR DESIRED STUDENTS

This league of eight Northeastern schools that had agreed to refrain from competing for athletes provided a framework for formation in 1958 of The Ivy Overlap Group to prevent price competition for *all* applicants for admission. The stated purpose of the group was to insure the applicants pay "approximately the same amount regardless of the Ivy Group institution they choose to attend." Stanford and Massachusetts Institute of Technology, though not members of the athletic league but perceived as direct competitors for college applicants, were invited to join.

MIT accepted the invitation. Stanford declined, stating that participants would be violating the Sherman Act, a federal criminal statute that prohibits, with provision for fines and imprisonment for violators, agreements between competitors that may affect price.

An athletic league to preserve sports competition between real college students rather than school-sponsored professional athletes provided a foundation on which to form a tuition price-fixing cartel. From agreement not to compete on price for athletes it was an easy step to agreement on prohibition of price competition for

ANY student. The result is a cartel that prevents price competition and denies to students any opportunity to choose between the schools in the league on the basis of price.

The schools formalized their agreement in a written manual. Meetings were held several times a year to insure that proposed discounts were evened out before being offered to an applicant who had applied to and had been accepted at more than one school. Deceptive terminology has prolonged public failure to understand what is happening. Cartel members are portrayed as engaged in charitable activity by the use of the term "financial aid" to refer to secret discriminatory discounts from the announced tuition price. "Financial aid" is not financial aid. It is simply a record kept of money not received.

"FINANCIAL AID" IS NOT A CHARITABLE GIFT TO THE NEEDY; IT IS A PRICE DISCOUNT GRANTED TO ATTRACT A CUSTOMER

To understand how the cartel works it is necessary to avoid the confusion generated by terms used by the academic establishment. "Financial aid" suggests generosity and charity toward the needy when in fact it is a secret discriminatory discount, or a lower price, offered to a desired customer. "Need blind admission" means that the admission decision includes the decision as to price to be paid after a conclusion is reached as to how much the customer can pay. Granting discounts for being a superior student — "merit scholarships" — would destroy the system, so such scholarships have been prohibited altogether by agreement of members of the cartel.

There is no way to measure the value or quality of what Yale is selling. Its product is a piece of paper with the trademark "Yale" on it. On Old Yale's diploma the president and faculty certified that the named individual had received a superior education. Only those adequately prepared were admitted as students. Only those who could, and did, absorb a basic liberal education received diplomas.

Today's Yale is trading on the reputation that Old Yale established. It is still possible to obtain a good education at today's Yale, but it is not required for a diploma. The curriculum has been diluted and standards have been lowered, but the trademark on the diploma is no less valuable. Nor has the price people are willing to pay for it. What is being bought is the brand on a piece of paper.

MAINTAINING THE VALUE OF THE BRAND

To maintain its valuable brand, today's Yale publishes its "acceptance rate" — percentage of applicants accepted for admission — and its "yield" — percentage of those accepted who enroll. Efforts are made to show high percentages of the latter and low percentages of the former. Yale has an elaborate structure of staff and energetic alumni that encourages applicants to apply for admission regardless of their records or potential.

The *Yale Daily News* has reported that "the University has recently deployed a mailing system whereby it sends two postcards and a letter at three separate stages of the application process to high school students who have scored highly on standardized tests and who live in zip codes where the median family earns less than $65,000. Each postcard informs students about Yale's application process and the school's financial aid packet." Keeping the number of applicants up helps to keep the acceptance rate low, which maintains prestige on which the value of the brand depends.

In colleges, as in country clubs, exclusivity adds value independent of the quality of the product. People want to go where not everyone can. With products the quality of which cannot be objectively measured but depend on subjective appeal, such as perfume and whiskey, a higher price itself can add additional value to the product — the higher the price, the more prestigious the product. The more money that some pay to obtain a Yale diploma, the more value the diploma has to anyone who can get one.

ALL QUESTIONS ARE OPEN QUESTIONS; ALL MANNER OF BEHAVIOR IS ACCEPTABLE

In a speech to incoming freshman, class of 2012, in August 28, Yale's president told the students they would "have complete freedom to explore, learn about new subjects, meet new people, and pursue new passions." He urged them to "be adventurous and dare to be different."

PRICE DISCRIMINATION FACILITATES TUITION INCREASES

The economists and financiers who run today's Yale know that, to maintain its prestigious trademark, it is better to raise the announced tuition price and grant more discounts than to lower the price but grant fewer discounts. Equal revenue can be obtained either way from those who receive the discounts. Increased revenue is obtained from those who pay the full sticker price. The diploma's value is enhanced by keeping the sticker price up.

Yale, like most of its direct competitors with low acceptance rates and high yields, has raised its announced price beyond what most students whom Yale wants can pay. Rather than continue a price announced as available to all applicants, the school is able to raise the announced price but grant secret individually-tailored lower prices to those who can demonstrate that Yale is extracting the maximum available from the student's family resources, confident that none of the other members of the cartel will beat its offer. Applicants will be given no opportunity to choose between schools on the basis of price.

THE CARTEL DENIES APPLICANTS ANY CHOICE BASED ON PRICE

To avoid frightening away possible applicants by a higher announced tuition, today's Yale encourages applicants to believe that their financial situation makes no difference to their chances for being admitted. Consideration of the application is said to be "need-blind." If Yale decides to compete for the applicant, a secret discount sufficient to allow the student to attend is offered. To prevent a potential customer from shopping for discounts, the cartel agreement insures that no member of the cartel will offer any greater discount.

Today's Yale competes for superior students and for members of ethnic groups needed to maintain diversity goals, but, as a member of the Ivy League Cartel, it does not compete with other members of the league on price.

Sixty-four percent of undergraduates receive some form of "financial aid." The *Yale Daily News* quotes William Deresiewicz, a former Yale professor as saying that students that receive financial aid tend to come from upper middle class or white-collar families. "Most of the kids who receive financial aid may not come from plutocratic families, but doctors and lawyers need help paying for Yale too."

CHAPTER VII

Preservation of the Cartel

THE CARTEL IS SAVED BY POLITICS

From 1958 to 1989 the Ivy League Cartel operated without interference from government, allowing the schools to make substantial tuition increases with little risk that price competition would break out among them, but following a lengthy investigation, the staff of the Antitrust Division recommended to the US Attorney General Richard Thornburg that he file a civil suit seeking an injunction.

Theoretically under the law the staff could have recommended criminal proceedings with the potential of fine and imprisonment, since the facts could not be disputed and the violation was clear. Before doing anything, Thornburg decided to discuss the matter with the president of Harvard, Derek Bok.

Thornburg asked Bok whether Harvard might agree to change what it was doing. Bok, who had taught antitrust law at Harvard, took the position that Harvard knew more about education than the Department of Justice; that Harvard was not doing anything illegal; and that it was not going to change anything. That left Thornburg little choice in dealing with his staff's recommendation.

Thornburg could not ignore the recommendation. He filed a civil action seeking an injunction. The suit was filed in the US District Court in Philadelphia in 1991, naming all eight Ivy League schools and Massachusetts Institute of Technology, and alleging that the defendants had unlawfully conspired to restrain trade in violation of Section 1 of the Sherman Act.

The litigation went on for years. All defendants except M.I.T. consented to a judgment enjoining them from fixing "financial aid;" M.I.T. chose to defend.

In September of 1992, after a trial without a jury, Chief Judge L.C. Bechtle issued a decision and order, 805 F.Supp. 288 (E.D.Pa.1992). M.I.T. was found to have violated the law and was "enjoined from entering into ... any combination or conspiracy which has the effect, or the tendency to affect, the determination of the price, or any adjustment thereof, expected to be paid by, or on behalf of, a prospective student, whether identified as tuition, family contribution, financial aid awards, or some other component of the cost of providing the student's education by the institutions to which the student has been admitted." M.I.T. promptly appealed.

Judge Bechtle made detailed findings of fact to support his order. He cited provisions in the manual of the Council of Ivy League Presidents that the stated purpose of the Ivy Overlap Group was "to neutralize the effect of financial aid" so that "families will be asked to pay approximately the same amount regardless of the Ivy Group institution they choose to attend."

He found that

> "There were three main features of the Ivy Group process: all member institutions agreed to

(1) award financial aid solely on the basis of applicants' demonstrated financial need, and not on the basis of academic or athletic ability; (2) jointly develop and apply a uniform needs analysis formula for assessing applicants' expected family contributions; and (3) jointly determine and apply the family contribution determinations of commonly admitted students on a case-by-case basis."

The Group met approximately four times a year.

Judge Bechtle described the Spring meeting as follows:

"The Spring Meeting lasted two days. The multilateral meetings were chaired by a 'driver,' who called out each applicant's name and the schools which had admitted that applicant. The schools would than compare their own separately calculated family contribution figures with the other admitting schools' figures for that applicant. More often than not, the family contribution determinations made by the various schools prior to the Spring Meeting were similar. The similarity resulted from the fact that, for the most part, each school used the identical needs analysis formula. Family contribution differences of less than $500 were understood to be close enough not to warrant any discussion aimed at arriving at a common figure. Where there were significant differences (in excess of $500), the schools would either agree upon a common figure or agree to meet somewhere at or near the middle of the divergent figures. Each institution adopted and used these agreed-upon family contribution determinations in making their financial aid awards, and expected the other institutions to do likewise."

Judge Bechtle found that the schools did not make a genuine effort to assess the aid applicant's actual financial circumstances but that the figures agreed upon were the result of "compromise" and "expediency."

He also found the following:

"The only other institution of higher education that provided the Ivy Overlap Group with any meaningful competition for students was Stanford. The Ivy Overlap Group schools attempted to recruit Stanford into the group for fear that Stanford was luring high caliber students with merit scholarships and larger aid awards. Stanford refused the invitation upon its belief that Overlap violated the antitrust laws."

Judge Bechtle found that compliance with the agreement was policed and that cheating by the conspirators was rare. Violations provoked complaints. In October 1986, Princeton began awarding "research grants" to undergraduates without regard to need. As a result of complaints from the other schools, Princeton agreed to abandon the practice.

THE JUDGE FOUND THE SCHOOLS' ARGUMENT TO BE "PURE SOPHISTRY"

M.I.T. contended that the activities of the Ivy Overlap Group did not constitute trade or commerce and, therefore were not subject to the Sherman Act. Judge Bechtle rejected that argument. He did not accept M.I.T.'s characterization of financial aid as "charity." He saw financial aid as a "discount off the price of college offered to financial aid recipients." He concluded that, "By agreeing upon aid applicants' families expected financial contribution, the Ivy Overlap Group schools were setting the price aid applicants and their families would pay for educational services" and that M.I.T.'s attempt to dissociate the Overlap process from the commercial aspects of higher education was "pure sophistry."

Judge Bechtle noted the explicit written agreement among the members of the Group "not to provide merit aid to any applicant." He pointed out that "the Ivy Overlap Group's agreed-upon ban on merit scholarships foreclosed the possibility that non-aid applicants could receive a discount based on any type of meritorious achievement.

Judge Bechtle concluded, "No reasonable person could conclude that the Ivy Overlap Agreements did not suppress competition." He emphasized, "the member institutions formed the Ivy Overlap Group for the very purpose of eliminating competition for students." He found, "the fundamental objective ... was to eliminate price competition among the members."

None of the judge's findings as to the facts were contested, nor could they be. M.I.T. sought to defend its activities in the same way that Bok had defended Harvard's — what it was doing was not prohibited by law.

That contention was continued on appeal to the United States Court of Appeals for the Third Circuit. The effort to preserve the cartel was supported by the higher education establishment. The following filed briefs in support of M.I.T.:

- The American Council on Education

- The Association of American Medical Colleges

- The Association of American Universities

- The Association of Catholic Colleges and Universities

- The College Board

- The Council of Independent Colleges

- The National Association of Independent Colleges and Universities

- The National Association of State Universities and Land-Grant Colleges

- The National Association of Student Financial Aid Administrators

- The National Association of Student Personnel Administrators.

THE LAW BEING VIOLATED FREQUENTLY RESULTS IN PROCEEDINGS ENDING IN FINES AND IMPRISONMENT

In the Sherman Act of 1890 Congress declared a federal crime "every contract, combination or conspiracy in restraint of trade or commerce among the several states or with foreign nations" punishable by fine and/or imprisonment. Every contract restrains some trade, so the law as written would have made criminals of anyone who enters into a contract. Unable to acknowledge that the statute makes no sense, courts have struggled ever since to give meaning to this declaration.

In 1911, the Supreme Court rewrote the statute to apply only to contracts that "unreasonably" restrain trade. Antitrust lawyers refer to this as the "rule of reason," although it is impossible to state what conduct violates the rule. The doctrine is that not all agreements that restrain trade are anti-competitive. If they are not anti-competitive, they do not unreasonably restrain trade and are, therefore, not unlawful.

Rule-of-reason consideration opens up inquiry as to the effects of the agreement. Courts have developed doctrinal variations on the application of the "rule" that can involve the question of who has the burden of proof. There is an "abbreviated" or "quick look" rule of reason analysis and a "full-scale" rule of reason analysis. Under the rule of reason, almost everything is relevant and nothing is determinative.

The Supreme Court has declared, without any basis in fact or reason, its intuition that any agreement affecting price is anti-competitive, (without any proof of any facts as to the effect, if any, of the agreement), therefore unreasonable and, therefore, unlawful. Antitrust lawyers call this "per se" illegality. If the determination of "per se" illegality is not adopted, the courts turn to the rule of reason. There may then follow extended litigation over the facts and the issue for the judge is one of public policy.

Under Supreme Court precedents, Judge Bechtle might have accepted the Government's contention that the activities of the Ivy Overlap Group were illegal per se, since they affected price, but he did not. Instead, "in the exercise of caution and in light of the Supreme Court's repeated counsel against presumptive invalidation of restraints involving professional associations," he considered them by the rule of reason. He concluded that they violated the Sherman Act because he was not satisfied with M.I.T.'s asserted justification for what it was doing.

In his 2004 book, *Going Broke By Degree — Why College Costs Too Much,* Richard Vedder wrote: "Until the U.S. Justice Department intervened in the early 1990s representatives of top universities met to discuss individual students in devising scholarship strategies. The Justice Department considered that a form of price-fixing, and the universities reluctantly agreed to desist from the practice."

THE CARTEL CONTINUES ITS CONSPIRACY TO AVOID PRICE COMPETITION

Mr. Vedder missed the point. It was not just the Justice Department that considered the meetings to avoid competitive tuition offers price-fixing. So did a United States District Court judge after a full trial to establish the facts. The schools agreed to desist from further meetings since meetings were no longer necessary to ensure the continued effectiveness of the cartel. An exchange of letters left the schools free to continue their agreement not to grant merit scholarships. These letters, while available to the public upon request received no public attention or understanding.

A three-judge panel of the court of appeals heard argument of the appeal in June 1992, and issued its decision in September. (5 F.3d 658 (3d Cir. 1993)) The court was divided. One judge did not accept the characterization of financial aid as a price discount. He saw financial aid as "charity" given to "needy" students. He would not apply the Sherman Act to such activities. He would have granted judgment in favor of M.I.T.

Two judges, (a majority and, thus, "the court"), decided to return the matter to the district court for further proceedings. The court accepted Judge Bechtle's conclusion that the Overlap Group's activities were commercial and subject to the Sherman Act prohibition, concluding that "financial assistance to students is part and parcel of the process of setting tuition and thus a commercial transaction."

The court's opinion includes rococo legal reasoning, dressed up with citations of prior decisions, of how the rule of reason applies to this case. The court concluded that the Overlap Agreement is a "price fixing mechanism impeding the ordinary functioning of the free market," that M.I.T. "is obliged to provide justification for the arrangement," and that, since Judge Bechtle had made no conclusive findings as to the effects of the price fixing, the matter should be returned to him to do so.

The action of the court of appeals kept the case alive, but the prospect of Judge Bechtle's rewriting his findings cannot have been attractive to those who wished to preserve the cartel. They were saved from this fate by the presidential election in the fall of 1992 that changed control of the White House and the Department of Justice.

In December 1993, the Antitrust Division washed out the case with the acceptance of a letter from a lawyer for M.I.T. in which he reserved the right of the school to "agree to provide only need-based financial aid and to prohibit merit scholarships." The letter was phrased in such a way as to include any schools who choose to participate, not just those in the Overlap Group. By agreement the court case was dismissed.

THE SYSTEM IN PLACE TODAY MAKES SAVING BY A PARENT OR GRANDPARENT FOR YALE TUITION SENSELESS

Herschel Grossman, a professor of economics at Brown University wrote in January of 1994:

> "The recent decision by the Justice Department to drop its antitrust case against the Ivy League colleges and MIT shows the political clout of our elite educational institutions. It also means that these colleges will be able to collude again to restrict financial aid and to deny undergraduates the benefits of merit scholarships."

Grossman added:

> "In defending their cartel, MIT and the Ivy colleges argue that they are already budgeting about the maximum amount of money for financial aid they can afford. Hence, if competition were to force them to offer merit scholarships, they would have to decrease financial aid to needy students.

> "This argument is specious. The richest Ivy colleges (Harvard, Yale and Princeton) have substantially larger income from endowments and annual gifts than the other Ivy colleges and MIT. But the

richest colleges devote a smaller fraction of their gross revenue to financial aid for undergraduates.

"This anomaly suggests that collusion enables the richer participants to give less financial aid than they would give under competition.

"The not-for-profit designation allows colleges to keep their books in such a way that they report no profits. But this bookkeeping contrivance doesn't mean that colleges don't earn what an economist would properly call profits. Rather, it means that they include in what they call their costs some amounts that are really profits.

"In fact, private colleges function similarly to producer cooperatives or partnerships. The partners — in this case the faculty and administrators — share any excess revenue in the form of generous compensation and perquisites."

Professor Vance H. Fried of Oklahoma State University, writing in 2011 made the same point as follows:

"Undergraduate education is a highly profitable business for nonprofit colleges and universities. They do not show profits on their books, but instead take their profits in the form of spending on some combination of research, graduate education, low-demand majors, low faculty teaching loads, excess compensation, and featherbedding. The industry's high profits come at the expense of students and taxpayer. (Cato Policy Analysis No. 678, June 15, 2011)

In the words of Professor Grossman:

"The larger a family's income and savings, and the fewer children it has, the smaller the amount of need-based aid for which it qualifies. In this way, need-based financial aid penalizes industrious and thrifty families who have worked, saved and limited family size in order to be able to pay to send their children to college.

"In short, need-based financial aid encourages sensible families to be imprudent."

In 1966, Yale announced its policy of so-called "need-blind" admissions and "need-based" tuition discounts. Whether an applicant is admitted depends on Yale's diversity and social engineering goals, not family finances. As Yale puts it:

"Yale's financial aid is solely need-based. Our financial aid office will work to determine your parents' financial need and meet 100% of that need for all four years of study. We understand that each family has unique circumstances that may warrant consideration for family assistance."

This means that money saved by parents in advance for possible tuition fees later at Yale simply ensures more money will flow into Yale's investments. If the family of an applicant that Yale wants has less money than the sticker price requires, a secret discriminatory discount may be allowed.

In 2009, the president told the alumni magazine, "There has been a steady progression of more generous financial aid." And why wouldn't there be? Standards for demonstrating "need" (or what assets does the family have for Yale to draw on), have been developed since the cartel was established. Now there is a common form for establishing "need," the form used to apply for Government aid. Meetings, like the Spring meeting described by Judge Bechtle, to even out proposed discounts based on need are no longer necessary. The schools accepted a prohibition of further such meetings. In its press release announcing dismissal of the suit, the Government portrayed this preservation of the cartel as a victory. It was a way of reversing the previous DOJ decision to bring the suit without saying so.

Basic props of the cartel are now not only not under attack. They have received implied Government endorsement.

An exchange of letters has effectively granted approval by the antitrust authorities of agreements "to provide only need-based financial aid" and "to prohibit merit scholarships," the very things that the suit was brought to prevent and that the District Judge found violated the Sherman Act. (*Justice Department Settles MIT Price Fixing Case,* DOJ Press Release, 12/12/93, Appendix B; letter of Thane D. Scott, counsel for MIT, 12/22/93, to Robert E. Litan, Deputy AAG, Antitrust Div, US DOJ, with attached "Standards of Conduct," Appendix C).

As Judge Bechtle understood, this means continued stifling of price competition. By agreeing not to grant any discounts greater than "needed," the schools have agreed to grant no greater discounts than each other. Substantial tuition increases have followed since the schools have the incentive to increase revenue by continually raising the sticker price with commensurate discounts, confident that the other schools will follow.

In January 2008, Harvard announced changes in its discount system, indicating who might be granted how much discount from its then-$45,620 per year sticker price. When asked what Yale planned to do, the president said, "Wait until next week … I don't think once we've made these changes, any student will choose Harvard over Yale based on cost." ("Yale to Use More Endowment Funds," *Wall Street Journal,* 1/8/08, p. D-3.).

In 1994 Congress adopted a limited temporary exemption of "institutions of higher education" from the antitrust laws with regard to "need-based" "financial aid." The provision has been extended several times. It is now scheduled to expire in September 2015. The statute makes no reference to merit scholarships and has no bearing on the illegality of agreements not to grant them.

The system ensures mopping up any additional aid provided by government. (Gary Wolfram, "Making College More Expensive — The Unintended Consequence of Federal Tuition Aid," Policy Analysis No. 531, 1/25/05, Cato Institute.) When government increases aid, the schools increase tuition to capture it.

Over one ten-year period, the salary of Yale University's president was increased by nearly 300 percent.

CHAPTER VIII

Yale Today —
Light, Truth and Whatever

THE DEATH OF OLD YALE

O ld Yale, Mother of Men, was jackets and ties in the dining halls, "Mister" between professor and student, and a curriculum that included the basics in Western Civilization. The new Yale, today's Yale, is a cafeteria of 95 subjects of instruction from accounting to women's, gender and sexuality, (set out in a 700-page catalog). Yale College today is young men and women without adult supervision.

What happened at Yale was probably little different from what happened generally in American academic life. According to Joseph Epstein, WSJ5/28/14,

> "demographic diversity has triumphed over intellectual standards and the display of virtue over the search for truth. ... No serious university could do business without an African-American Studies Department. Many female professors created and found an academic home in something called

Gender Studies, which turned out to be chiefly about the suppression of women, just as African-American Studies was chiefly about the historical and contemporary mistreatment of blacks. ... Over time, the themes of gender, class and race were insinuated into the softer social sciences and much of the humanities."

Yale College is 1300 young men and women thrown together for four years to do as they please in comfortable surroundings. During the 2012-2013 academic year, a fifth of undergrads who responded to university surveys said they had blacked out due to alcohol at least once in the previous two weeks. Today's Yale, "the Gay Ivy," is Bladderball, Sex Week, a Saybrook College master who collects child pornography, fraternity candidates shouting obscenities, and a student working alone through the night catches her hair in a lathe and is strangled to death because she does not know how to turn off the power.

In April 2014 the *Yale Daily News* contained the following story: "Students dining in Commons on Thursday witnessed a male student dressed as a pregnant woman pretending to give birth on a Commons table with help of a fake midwife ... as members of the junior class sought to fulfill their induction requirements for Yale's secret societies."

TODAY'S YALE REFUSES TO PROVIDE A COURSE IN WESTERN CIVILIZATION

There is no longer an identifiable "Yale education." It is now, as the current president says, "the Yale Experience." The handling of the Bass gift defines nicely what has become of education at today's Yale.

In 1991, Benno Schmidt, who was then president of the university, solicited from Lee Bass '79 a gift of $20 million to be used for establishing a program in Western Civilization. Inspiration had come from Donald Kagan, a classics professor then Dean of Yale College. Schmidt and Kagan drew up the planned courses, including a mandatory one for first-year students similar to that required at Columbia.

Schmidt and Kagan were replaced. Naomi Riley, WSJ 10/13/07, described what happened:

> "Between 1991 and 1995, Mr. Bass repeatedly sought assurance that his money wouldn't be dumped into multicultural education. He kept asking the university's president, Richard Levin, when the program would materialize. When it became clear that the liberal faculty's objections to Mr. Bass's gift had won the day, he asked for his money back."

In a letter dated March 23, 1995, addressed to university alumni Levin announced return of the Bass gift. He said that he had to do this because Bass was attempting to insert himself into the selection of faculty to teach in the program. "To have honored this new request would have been contrary to the tradition and practices of this and other leading universities in our nation. The university must continue to use its own judgment of excellence in scholarship and teaching as the sole basis for faculty appointments." In other words, the club of tenured faculty that controls what the curriculum will be must also be allowed to control who teaches it without regard to what loyal and generous alumni might wish and be willing to pay for.

In his letter, Levin made no mention of the fact that Bass had requested return of the $20 million. Faculty ideologically opposed to the proposed Western Civilization program derailed it. Kagan was called a racist and peddler of European cultural arrogance. He later said, "The other side won." The other side was a faculty that dominated the president — feminists, Marxists, cultural relativists, and adherents of political correctness for whom there is no such thing as Western Civilization.

Schmidt has since written:

> "The greatest threat to academic freedom today is not outside the academy, but from within. … The assumption seems to be that the purpose of education is to induce correct opinion rather than to search for wisdom and to liberate the mind."
> *WSJ* 7/31/13

TODAY'S YALE HAS NO SENSE OF PURPOSE OR REASON FOR BEING

Old Yale was run by alumni of the college who were proud of its history. In his column "Yale, Inc." in the *Yale Daily News* Scott Stern, a junior in Branford College, has pointed out that today's Yale Corporation includes "the CEO of Pepsi, the CEO of Chanel, the CEO of Time Warner, the former CEO of Goodyear, the former CEO of Palm Computing (makers of the Palm Pilot), and the former CEO of J.P. Morgan. … [and that} … Yale has truly become a moneymaking institution… [with a] … corporate ideology … beyond the almost fetishistic reverence for the endowment."

Today's Yale is run by Stanford graduates, lawyers and financial manipulators who have no definite educational purpose, whose goal is maximization of revenues through worldwide exploitation of the brand. What began as a college for "education of suitable youth" has become a multi-billion dollar secret hedge fund without publicly-identified owners.

In its Form 990 for 2007, required to be filed with the Internal Revenue Service in order to retain tax-exempt status for its income and tax deductions for donors, Yale University stated its "primary exempt purpose" as "education, research, community service." The form for 2011 required a description of "the organization's most significant activities." The university omitted any use of the word "education" and responded with "To create, preserve and disseminate knowledge."

For the year ending June 30, 2012, Yale stated its net assets or fund balances as 20 billion dollars. There is little disclosure as to the basis for this figure or of where the assets are or of how their evaluation was arrived at.

The university appears to be supported by three main revenue streams — 1) contributions and grants, 2) program service revenue, and 3) investment income, plus 77 million dollars in 2012 of "other revenue."

Yale University employs a professional staff of fundraisers. There is a University Director of an Office of Planned Giving with a Deputy Director and three Planned Giving Specialists. Yale reported 37.5 million dollars were spent on "fundraising" during fiscal 2012.

There is no direct relationship between any of the three main revenue streams and the quantity or quality of the product being sold. Yale University runs a college to make money by exploiting a brand. It is helped to do so by membership in a cartel with its closest competitors that agree to refrain from tuition price competition. Government action to break up the cartel was dropped to accommodate those who benefit financially from its continuance.

CHAPTER IX

A Bloated Yale — Generous or Greedy?

S o Old Yale, Mother of Men, no longer exists, having been replaced by a money-guzzler with no identifiable purpose other than its own continued existence, holding a large portfolio of secret investments. Scholarships are no longer a reward for being a scholar but are part of a deceptive scheme of price discrimination. So what?

Most of those who might regret the death of Old Yale are dead, but anyone who is concerned about the cost of college education in the United States should look closely at what is happening at Yale. The Ivy League Cartel, of which Yale is a charter member, has for decades persistently raised the price to attend a member school. These increases have provided an umbrella over increases at other schools. The Ivy League has been a pacesetter in the race of the education establishment to gouge students and taxpayers.

HOW HAVE THE IVIES BEEN ABLE TO DO WHAT THEY HAVE DONE?

According to prevailing economic theory, price, (whether of automobiles or of college education), is determined by supply and demand. A market price is arrived at by the match of the highest price at which most prospective buyers are willing to buy with the lowest price at which sellers are willing to sell. The process is thought to best allocate resources and to exert pressure on sellers to keep their costs and prices low, with consequent public benefit.

This law of economics does not apply to Yale tuition the way it does to the price of automobiles.

To understand why, one must understand what Yale is selling. Yale is selling not only a cafeteria of college courses and four years of comfortable living in New Haven, ("the Yale Experience" in the words of the current president), but also a valuable brand on a piece of paper. There are many other places in the United States where the prospective buyer can obtain equally high quality education and residential accommodations. There is only one place where one can obtain a diploma stamped "Yale." That is in New Haven.

YALE CHOOSES ITS CUSTOMERS

Unlike General Motors' sales of automobiles, Yale's sales of branded diplomas with four years' room and board are limited in number each year. Yale has only so many to sell. The number is fixed by the size of the physical plant. GM wishes to sell as many autos as buyers will buy, and the more buyers there are, the more autos GM produces. (Yale is building more residential facilities and has franchised an operation in Singapore, but these moves have no effect on current prices.)

GM sells to anyone who wishes to buy. Yale chooses its customers. The last time there were fewer buyers for Yale's product than

Yale could offer to sell was in 1932. The situation was promptly remedied, not by lowering price, but by lowering admission standards. The number of applicants for admission to the next freshman year rose sufficiently to fill the class and has exceeded it every year since. Today's Yale has many applicants from which to choose.

The *Yale Daily News* has reported that the Ivies "are obligated by the Common Ivy League Agreement to release their [admission] decisions on the same day." This assists in maintenance of the cartel, keeping members in line and not jumping the gun in bidding for potential buyers.

For the class of 2018 Yale offered admission to 1,935 applicants, or 6.26% of 30,932 who applied. (The previous year Yale accepted 1,991 out of 29,610, or 6.72%.) With so many potential customers eager to buy, Yale is under no pressure to keep tuition low. If GM raises price, it may lose sales. Not so with Yale. It need have little concern about losing buyers by raising price. It is turning buyers away by the thousands.

ECONOMIC LAWS THAT BENEFIT THE PUBLIC DO NOT APPLY TO YALE

Who owns Yale? People tend to assume that Yale is a charitable institution, supported by generous benefactors, run by public servants following the noble profession of educating the young. Yale University is a "non-profit" organization and is exempt from income taxation. Gifts to Yale may be deducted by donors from their taxable income as gifts to "charity." Yale receives a substantial stream of such gifts.

The people running Yale College no longer have any shared idea of what education is or that there is any such thing. Yale education today has no fixed content Yale is primarily a research institution, the guiding philosophy of which is that all questions are open questions, (except those closed by the requirements of political correctness), that there is no body of knowledge or values that should be taught to the young.

YALE IS RICH

General Motors is required by law to make public periodic reports of its finances. The owners of Yale hold very closely their financial records. They make no disclosure of budgets: past, present or future. The only public disclosure of Yale's financial information is that contained in the Form 990, required to be filed annually with the Internal Revenue Service in order to preserve tax favoritism. The reports are not those used by the managers to run the organization. Yale regularly requests extensions of time to make the required filing.

The reports are specially prepared for disclosure from internal documents not disclosed, and are accompanied by self-congratulatory promotional rhetoric. Unlike corporate reports required to be filed at the Securities & Exchange Commission without delay, Yale's reports are usually not released until seven or eight months after the end of the fiscal year. The date for filing the report for the period ending June 30, 2013, was extended to February 15, 2014.

Yale is required by law to furnish a copy of its completed Form 990 to anyone who requests it. Requesters receive a package of papers each page of which is headed "Public Disclosure Copy." There is no indication how this may differ from the copy actually filed or what pages, if any, have been omitted.

As of June 30, 2013, Yale University reported net assets of $21,937,281,633. Total revenue of approximately $3.6 billion less total expenses of approximately $3.3 billion left net revenue of $370 million for the year. The list of "expenses" contains no reference to "financial aid," since financial aid is not an expense but a discount. It is not money paid out but simply money not received. There is no public disclosure of where Yale's billions are. For 2012, Yale reported owning $116 million in "common stock," $18.9 billion in "equity investments" and $202 million in "other investments," all measured by "end of the year market value."

Little of Yale's spending goes for instruction. Much goes to administration, executive management, comfortable facilities, legal and fiscal services, and public relations. During fiscal year ending June 30, 2013, Yale spent $43.8 million on travel, $3 million on advertising and promotion, and $97.3 million on investment management fees. During the same period, Yale gave $50 million to governments and organizations in the U.S.; $326 million to individuals in the U.S.; and $17.4 million to government, organizations and individuals outside the U.S.

All of these "grants" were called "expenses." Commanding such riches, Yale can comfortably refuse to accept a gift of $20 million conditioned on offering a course in western civilization.

Yale's owners are generous to themselves in salaries, pensions and perquisites, but tenacious in collective bargaining with kitchen and maintenance workers and resolute in desire to maximize revenue. When student environmentalists urged Yale to remove non-green stocks from it investment portfolio, Yale refused without hesitation.

In an interview with a *Wall Street Journal* editorial board member in June 2009, the president of Yale said: "We're non-profits. We're not supposed to accumulate large surpluses." Yale raised tuition that year 3.2%. The accumulated surplus grew from $3.1 billion in 1993 to $23 billion in 2008. Yale's net worth of 20-plus billion dollars has been built by persistent tuition rises, gifts from generous and gullible alumni and U.S. taxpayers.

THE IN-GROUP DOES WELL FOR ITSELF

Total compensation in 2012 paid to Yale's in-house lawyer was $1,666,175, up from 615,286 in 2011. That same year one Vice-president received $1,748,767, up from $694,656 in 2011. The president received total compensation in 2011 of $1,652,523 and raised it in 2012 to $1,840,284.

YALE STRIVES TO INCREASE ITS RICHES

Not content with wealth nearly ten times its total annual expenses, Yale tries to increase its riches by raising tuitions, milking alumni, seeking more government money for research, and by making creative investments. Having sufficient money, (pretentiously called "the endowment"), and reliable revenue streams to continue operations in perpetuity, and not content with earnings that might be expected from ordinary safe investments, Yale's owners decided to use some of their money to make more money by making more risky investments.

At the end of 2007, Yale had 11% of its money in U.S. stocks, 14% in foreign stocks and 4% in bonds, and had put the larger percentage in "private equity." During a period when all boats were rising, this strategy produced phenomenal results. When the inevitable downturn occurred, Yale lost 25% of its net worth. One might ask why Yale is playing in this game

Today's Yale is rich in a way that Old Yale never was. The effective owners of this Yale enrich themselves and make bets in financial markets seeking to mass an even larger pile of accumulated surplus. Yale has gone from a college founded for the education of suitable youth to a hedge fund owned by and run for the benefit of those on the payroll. One might ask why the taxpayer should support this cycle in any way. Tax money is going, both directly and indirectly, to maintain a directionless research organization that provides no-content education to young people chosen for social engineering purposes.

THE FACULTY AND ADMINISTRATORS OWN YALE

The effective owners of the Yale brand are the tenured faculty and the chief administrators, subject to oversight by a group of volunteers known as "the Corporation." The president of Yale University is chosen by the Corporation and becomes a member of the Corporation. Except for the president, members of the Corporation are paid nothing for their time to attend meetings. To the contrary, they are frequently looked to for the contribution of substantial sums of money. They seek membership for the prestige.

Some members are elected for fixed terms by Yale alumni after demonstrating long and strong support for things as they are. The majority are appointed for life to replace a successor to an original trustee. Given the reason they serve and how they have been selected, they are not likely to rock the boat or to challenge actions of the owners of the brand.

There are two additional members of the Corporation, the governor and lieutenant governor of Connecticut. These individuals, selected by the voters of Connecticut and not insiders at Yale University, would be in a position to exercise some independent supervision over what goes on at Yale, but, according to Yale's latest filing with the Internal Revenue Service, "historically… [the governor and lieutenant governor]… do not participate in governance activities at the university."

Owners of General Motors want costs to go down so profits will go up and the value of their investment will increase. The owners of Yale have no similar desire to see costs go down and no incentive to lower them. In fact, their incentive is to increase costs. The majority of Yale's costs are the owners' salaries and those of their deputies and assistants and administrators and secretaries.

AN ILLEGAL CARTEL PREVENTS IVY LEAGUE PRICE COMPETITION

There is another reason why the present owners of the Yale brand can raise the price of a diploma without concern over possible loss of customers. As Judge Bechtle found, Yale has an agreement with its closest competitors that ensures that Yale's price will not be undercut in bidding for accepted applicants. This agreement was successfully attacked by the first Bush Administration as a clear-cut violation of the Sherman Act, but the result was washed out by the Clinton Administration's acceptance of a decree that permits the very thing the suit attacked.

Yale's announced tuition is so high that a majority of Yale's students do not have the family assets to pay it. If an applicant for admission to Yale is admitted to both Yale and another Ivy League college or M.I.T. but cannot pay the sticker price, Yale can be con-

78

fident that its competitor for the student will not offer a lower price to get the student because the other college has agreed in writing not to do so.

This has been accomplished by an agreement to offer only "financial aid," for need established by a fixed formula and, in no case on the basis of merit. "Merit" scholarships have been forbidden in the Ivy League by explicit written agreement since 1958.

CHAPTER X

The Fairy Tale of Financial Aid

T he United States District Court in Philadelphia understood
what most people now deploring the rise in college tuition
costs do not — how the system works and the deceptive
nature of the term "financial aid." The term "aid" suggests a gift
to those in need, like cash to the homeless or Thanksgiving and
Christmas dinners for the indigent. It is no such thing. There is no
gift, and there is no aid.

What is called "financial aid" is simply a secret discount allowed
to preferred customers. The recipient receives nothing. The seller
accepts a lower price than that advertised. The seller offers a lower
price to a particularly desired customer because another seller is
offering to do the same for that customer.

The system ensures that no applicant, rich or poor, will be given
a choice between schools in the cartel on the basis of cost to the student. As Yale's president said, "I don't think any student will choose
Harvard over Yale based on cost." He knew how the system works.

Observers call attention to the rising cost of college: (a) "1,225
percent since 1978, nearly twice the rate of the rise in health care
costs," and (b) "more than 1000 percent since the late 1990s while
the Consumer Price Index has risen only 240 percent" with conse-

quent student debt ($1.3 trillion). Confused by the deceptive term "financial aid" and handicapped by ignorance of how the system works, they suggest solutions that can only make the situation worse.

Thomas Sowell explained it all years ago in his book *Inside American Education* published in 1993:

> "Part of what is called "financial aid" in academia is simply a fancy name for a discount on paper, as it would be called more plainly and more honestly in ordinary commercial transactions, even transactions with used-car dealers. Where there is real money changing hands on behalf of students, that financial aid is largely provided by or guaranteed by, the federal government. ... The specific terms under which the government provides student financial aid virtually guarantees tuition escalation to unaffordable levels in private colleges and universities."

The "financial aid" fiction, used at all levels of U.S. education, with its pretense of charity serves to transfer wealth from the middle class and taxpayers of all classes to, in Yale's case, to the affluent owners of Yale. This is doubly unfortunate, since Yale's use of the scheme is buttressed by an illegal cartel and Yale has no use for the money anyway.

THE PROBLEM REQUIRES DEFINITION

The President of the United States has released a memo proposing a "Student Aid Bill of Rights" and is reported to be studying the idea for dealing with the problem of rising student loan defaults by making bankruptcy easier for those with student loans.

A pair of commentators in *The Wall Street Journal* note, "three quarters of a typical college budget is spent on personnel expenses, including benefits." They suggest "A Business Productivity Audit" that might lead to greater efficiency. This would put more money in the hands of administrators to do with as they please but have no effect on tuition.

Two commentators in The New York Times say, "no matter how high tuition climbs, there is always a federal loan to make up the difference between price and aid." They propose, "colleges should be made responsible for a portion of student-loan defaults."

Another commentator in *The New York Times* suggests, "a solution that can make college more accessible and affordable for middle-and-lower income students: Tuition Deferment. Colleges should offer alternative loan programs by allowing students to defer up to 75 percent of the cost of attending school — tuition, room, board and fees — and pay it back over 20 years." Instead of borrowing from banks, students should mortgage their futures to the school.

In 2008, Yale disclosed that 33% of Yale's operating expenses came out of accumulated surplus. The following year, it was 43%, (with 11% from tuitions).

When consideration was being given in the US Congress to require colleges such as Yale to spend more of their surplus, Yale disclosed that it had been "spending" less than 4% of its "endowment each year and planned in the future to go up to no less than 4.5% and no more than 6%. With annual returns on investment of more than 12 or 15 %, this was no threat to solvency. Yale's president muddied the waters of transparency by making this statement in the *Yale Alumni Magazine:* "Financial aid is not fully funded. Even with the increased endowment payout, we'll use more unrestricted funds to support financial aid next year."

When alumni gave money to old Yale for scholarships like mine, it was a gift that made my Yale education possible, and education at Yale had content and meaning. By giving money to today's Yale, the donor can have no effect on who is accepted for admission or what education, if any, they receive there.

As tuitions rise, more families become "needy." Politicians suggest more "aid" either of gifts or loans, making it easier for colleges to raise tuition again. The system of confusion and pretense will probably continue. Any efforts at change will meet determined resistance from tenured faculty and entrenched administrators.

They will fight hard against any interference with their complete freedom of action, under the banners of "academic freedom" and the pursuit of "diversity." They will be supported, as they were in the M.I.T. litigation, by the entire academic establishment, one of the most powerful lobbies in Washington.

Federal law contains a provision that state attorneys general can bring suits on behalf of the state's citizens injured by an antitrust law violation. Judge Bechtle's findings could provide a basis for such a suit. Identifying those injured and quantifying their damages would be difficult but not impossible. Perhaps an ambitious state attorney general will try it. And perhaps an energetic plaintiff class action lawyer will urge one to do so.

CHAPTER XI

What Should be Done?

There is no reason why any of the following should not be done.

FULL FINANCIAL DISCLOSURE SHOULD BE REQUIRED

Yale can no longer claim to be a private institution entitled to keep its financial affairs private. In fact, today's Yale regards itself as a sort of global quasi- public utility the mission of which is, in the words of the 2012 Form 990, "to attract a diverse group of … men and women from around the world and to educate them for leadership … in … society" regardless of the direction such leadership might lead. Timely financial reports should be publicly released so that those from whom the money comes, either willingly or by force of taxation, can see where it is going.

YALE'S TAX-EXEMPT STATUS SHOULD BE REVIEWED

Whether what Yale is doing qualifies as charity is open to question. Why should U.S. taxpayers be subsidizing "The Yale Experience" for young people from other countries?

THE SHERMAN ACT SHOULD BE ENFORCED AND THE IVY LEAGUE CARTEL BROKEN UP

The US Department of Justice prosecutes criminal proceedings against people who are doing what those controlling Yale are doing. We fine and send some of them to jail even when there is no clear evidence that their price-fixing has resulted in higher prices. It is impossible to ignore that Yale's prices have risen to an unconscionable extent.

There is no life left in Derek Bok's claim that Yale is not engaged in trade or commerce subject to the Sherman Act. The devious action of the Clinton Administration of quietly washing out the success of the first Bush Administration attacking it should be reversed.

###

United States v. Brown University, 805 F. Supp. 288 (E.D. Pa. 1992)

U.S. District Court for the Eastern District of Pennsylvania —
805 F. Supp. 288 (E.D. Pa. 1992)
September 2, 1992

805 F. Supp. 288 (1992)
UNITED STATES of America
v.
BROWN UNIVERSITY IN PROVIDENCE IN THE
STATE OF RHODE ISLAND AND PROVIDENCE
PLANTATIONS; the Trustees of Columbia University in
the City of New York; Cornell University; the Trustees of
Dartmouth College; President and Fellows of Harvard
College, Massachusetts; Massachusetts Institute of
Technology; the Trustees of Princeton University; the
Trustees of the University of Pennsylvania; and Yale
University.

Civ. A. No. 91-3274.

United States District Court, E.D. Pennsylvania.

September 2, 1992.

*289 Michael M. Baylson, U.S. Atty., Philadelphia, Pa., D. Bruce Pearson, Jessica N. Cohen, Jon B. Jacobs, Seymour H. Dussman, Michael P. Gaughan, Joseph H. Widmar, and Robert E. Bloch, U.S. Dept. of Justice, Washington, D.C., for plaintiff U.S.

Thane D. Scott, Robert E. Sullivan, Michael T. Gass, Bruce D. Berns, and Anita M. Polli, Palmer & Dodge, Boston, Mass., Andre L. Dennis, Stradley, Ronon, Stevens & Young, Philadelphia, Pa., for defendant Massachusetts Institute of Technology.

DECISION AND ORDER
BECHTLE, Chief Judge.

I. INTRODUCTION

The United States brought the instant action after a two-year investigation of the financial aid programs of various colleges and universities across the country. In its one-count verified complaint, the government alleged that the above-captioned defendants unlawfully conspired to restrain trade in violation of § 1 of the Sherman Act, 15 U.S.C. § 1 (1990), by collectively determining the amount of financial assistance awarded to students. The court entered final judgment against all defendants, with their consent, except for Massachusetts Institute of Technology which decided to defend against the charges. After a non-jury trial, the court renders the following decision:

II. FINDINGS OF FACT

1. Defendant, Massachusetts Institute of Technology ("MIT"), is a non-profit institution of higher education. MIT is incorporated under the laws of Massachusetts.

2. According to its charter, granted in 1861, MIT was incorporated:

[f]or the purpose of instituting and maintaining a society of arts, a museum of arts, and a school of industrial science, and aiding generally, by suitable means, the advancement, development and practical application of science in connection with arts, agriculture, manufactures and commerce....

3. MIT is governed by the MIT Corporation, over which the Chairman presides, and an Executive Committee. The MIT Corporation is comprised of 70 elected volunteer members, including distinguished leaders in science, engineering, industry, education and public service, and eight *ex officio* members. The Governor of Massachusetts, the Chief Justice of the Massachusetts Supreme Judicial Court, and the Massachusetts Commissioner of Education are all *ex officio* members of the MIT Corporation.

*290 4. The Executive Committee is comprised of ten members. Seven of those are drawn from the 70 elected volunteer board members and the other three are the Chairman, President and Treasurer of MIT. The Executive Committee is responsible for the oversight of MIT's operations.

5. MIT's operating budget is approximately $1.1 billion. MIT maintains an endowment of approximately $1.5 billion (which consistently ranks among the ten largest in the nation) and receives tuition payments and other income of approximately $158 million.

6. MIT offers undergraduate and graduate programs. MIT's educational programs are provided through five schools, engineer-

ing, science, architecture and planning, management, and humanities and social science.

7. Each year MIT receives several thousand applications, including many from students who are not Massachusetts residents, some of whom ultimately enroll at MIT. Many applications for admission are transported to MIT from other states. MIT receives money, including charitable donations and non-refundable application fees, from out-of-state residents.

8. The Ivy League is an organization made up of eight institutions of higher education. The eight Ivy League schools are Brown University, Columbia University, Cornell University, Dartmouth College, Harvard University, Princeton University, the University of Pennsylvania, and Yale University.

9. MIT and the Ivy League schools are included among the group of elite higher education institutions in the country. MIT and the Ivy League schools comprise the Ivy Overlap Group.

10. MIT has also been an associate member of the Pentagonal/Sisters Overlap Group, which included the five "Pentagonal" schools (Amherst, Williams, Wesleyan, Bowdoin, and Dartmouth), the "Seven Sisters" schools (Barnard, Bryn Mawr, Mount Holyoke, Radcliffe, Smith, Vassar, and Wellesely) and four other schools (Colby, Middlebury, Trinity, and Tufts).

MIT'S ADMISSION PRACTICES AND POLICIES

11. Each year MIT receives between six and seven thousand applications from prospective students. Approximately 2,000

students are admitted, approximately 1,100 of whom ultimately enroll.

12. In deciding whether to admit applicants, MIT evaluates the applicants' grades, class rank, performance on scholastic aptitude and achievement tests, the quality of their high school academic program, and personal accomplishments.

13. MIT seeks to admit very able students. For example, in the 1991-92 academic year, 259 of the 880 MIT freshmen who had high school ranks were class valedictorians, and 83% were in the top 5% of their high school classes. Of that same MIT entering class, 50% had math SAT scores above 750 (out of a possible 800) and 80% had math scores over 700. The average math SAT score for the 1992-1993 freshmen class was 735.

14. MIT's principal competitors for "high quality" undergraduate students are Harvard, Princeton, Stanford, and Yale.

15. For the 1991-92 academic year, the undergraduate enrollment was approximately 4,400 students.

16. MIT regularly conducts reply studies of its admitted students. In 1988, 82% of all students admitted to MIT attended MIT, another Ivy Overlap Group school, or Stanford. Eighty-eight percent of students admitted to MIT considered to be the "highest achievers" enrolled in these schools.

17. MIT employs a "need-blind admissions" system. Under this system, all admission decisions are based entirely on an applicant's merit, without any regard to the applicant's financial circumstances or ability to pay.

18. It is also MIT's policy to meet the full financial aid needs of attending students. When available resources do not meet students' financial need, MIT subsidizes the balance through additional assistance in the form of institutional grants.

*291 19. MIT's policies of need-blind admissions and need-based aid have allowed many students to attend MIT who, for a lack of financial resources, otherwise would not have been able to attend.

20. For the 1991-92 academic year, approximately 44% of the undergraduate enrollment were from American minority groups. By contrast, three decades ago, little more than 3% or 4% of MIT's undergraduate student body were from American minority groups.

21. For the 1991-92 academic year, 57% of students attending MIT received financial aid from MIT.

THE FINANCIAL AID PROCESS

22. Under the federal financial aid program, students and their families are expected to use their combined assets in order to finance the student's college education. *See* 20 U.S.C. §§ 1078(a) (2) and 1087mm (1989).

23. When family assets are insufficient to meet college expenses, the student becomes eligible for federal loans or loan guarantees. *See* 20 U.S.C. § 1078(a) (2), 1087kk and 1087mm.

24. In order to qualify for federally funded financial aid, students and their families must disclose financial information by completing the College Scholarship Service's ("CSS") Financial Aid Form ("FAF").

25. CSS is a branch of the College Board's Educational Testing Service. CSS functions as the principal processor for financial aid programs in the United States.

26. CSS collects financial information from aid applicants, processes that information using a standardized formula, and distributes that information to participating institutions. More than 2,000 colleges and universities rely on CSS for processing financial aid data.

27. The FAF solicits detailed information concerning the income and assets of financial aid applicants. This information includes the adjusted gross income of the student and his or her parents from the previous year's federal income tax return, the number of dependents, the number of family members enrolled in private elementary, secondary and post-secondary institutions, and the net assets of the student and the parents.

28. CSS processes the information on the FAF and sends the data to the United States Department of Education, which makes the initial calculation of each aid applicant's expected "family contribution."

29. The family contribution is the amount which the student and his or her family may be reasonably expected to contribute towards his or her educational expenses for one year. *See* 20 U.S.C. § 1087mm. The family contribution comprised of two parts: the parent contribution and the student contribution.

30. The Department of Education sends its family contribution determination back to CSS. CSS then incorporates the data into its Financial Aid Form Needs Analysis Report ("FAFNAR").

CSS sends the FAFNAR to the applicant and each school to which the applicant has applied.

31. Presently, the Department of Education determines family contribution by using the "Congressional Methodology," which is the needs analysis methodology required by the Higher Education Amendments of 1986 for the awarding of federally-funded or federally-guaranteed financial aid. *See* 20 U.S.C. § 1087nn, *et seq.*

32. Federal financial aid policy aims to ensure that similarly situated students are treated the same regardless of which institution, or aid officer within that institution, reviews their applications, and that students with less financial need do not receive more aid than those students with more financial need.

33. The Congressional Methodology became effective for the 1988-89 academic year. Prior to the enactment of the Congressional Methodology, CSS determined family contribution by applying the "Uniform Methodology," which was approved by the Department of Education as an acceptable methodology for distributing federal financial aid funds.

34. Under the Congressional Methodology, a school may either increase or decrease the Department of Education's family ***292** contribution determination by that school's using its "professional judgment."

35. A school is permitted to use its professional judgment when "special circumstances" exist. Professional judgment may be used on a case-by-case basis only; schools may not consider special circumstances that exist among a class of students. *See* 20 U.S.C. § 1087tt.

36. Professional judgment could be used, for example, if an institution's financial aid officer concluded that there was a significant change in the financial condition of a family, or if the cost for room and board turned out to be higher than was previously estimated.

37. Guidelines do not exist for the use of professional judgment. Various colleges may choose to apply professional judgment in different ways and under different circumstances. As a result, through the use of professional judgment, different schools may end up with divergent family contribution determinations with respect to the same applicant even though both schools used the Congressional Methodology.

38. The Department of Education recommends that professional judgment be used sparingly.

39. In addition to the information provided to CSS, individual schools may require applicants to provide additional financial information.

40. MIT requires its applicants to complete the MIT Financial Aid Application and submit copies of the applicants' and their parents' latest federal tax returns. In cases where the applicants' parents are divorced or separated, MIT requires the completion of a Divorced/Separated Parent's Statement.

41. MIT determines a student's "financial need" by subtracting its family contribution determination from the applicant's "student budget."

42. The student budget includes tuition, room and board, and other expenses such as books, materials, and travel.

43. MIT's current student budget is approximately $25,000.

44. There are two types of financial aid: grants and self-help.

45. Grants are financial assistance which the recipient is not required to repay.

46. Self-help is assistance in the form of loans or school-year employment opportunities. Each institution maintains its own self-help "level," which is the minimum amount all students are expected to provide themselves. Awards of self-help alone satisfy the demonstrated financial need of fewer than 9% of all aid recipients at MIT.

47. MIT's standard self-help level for the 1991-92 academic year was $6,100.

48. Students whose need exceeds the self-help levels require additional assistance. Approximately 91% of MIT aid recipients receive this additional assistance in the form of grants.

49. If a student receives any federal need-based aid, he or she may not receive additional aid from an institution which would exceed his or her need as calculated under the Congressional Methodology. Such aid is considered an "overaward."

50. If a student receives one dollar from a federal need-based aid program, all financial aid funds provided to that student must be awarded on the basis of need.

OVERLAP PROCESS

51. The Ivy Overlap Group was created in 1958 by MIT and the Ivy League schools. The purpose of the Ivy Overlap Group is

set forth in the Manual of the Council of Ivy League Presidents ("Manual").

52. Under the caption "Financial Aid policies and procedures," the Manual states the following:

1. Member institutions agree that the primary purpose of a college financial aid program for all students is to provide financial assistance to students who without such aid would be unable to attend that institution. Financial aid should only be awarded after it is determined that family resources are inadequate to meet the student's educational expenses, and such aid should not exceed the difference between educational expenses and family resources. *293 MIT is considered a member of the Ivy Group for purposes of these rules.

2. Ivy Group institutions follow the common policy that any financial aid shall be awarded solely on the basis of demonstrated need. Moreover, in order to insure that financial awards to commonly admitted candidates are reasonably comparable, all Ivy Group institutions will share financial information concerning admitted candidates in an annual "Ivy Overlap" meeting just prior to the mid-April common notification date. *The purpose of the compare agreement is to neutralize the effect of financial aid so that a student may choose among Ivy Group institutions for non-financial reasons.*

   a. *Family contributions shall be compared and adjusted if necessary so that, as a general rule, families will be asked to pay approximately the same amount regardless of the Ivy Group institution they choose to attend.* As a result, total financial need should differ by the approximate amount that costs at the respective institutions differ. Also, subject to variations in individual institutional financial aid policy, there is a further goal of establishing a balance between scholarship and self-help that is roughly comparable.

b. Member institutions shall continue to compare late awards and adjustment to awards after the formal overlap session until the student decides which college he or she will attend.

3. So that the process of comparing financial aid awards among member institutions can be facilitated, Ivy Group financial aid directors shall meet as necessary to agree on the basic principles of a financial needs analysis system. In particular they shall agree on a common system for measuring parental ability to pay and also seek to reduce differences in the other elements of needs analysis such as: contributions from student assets and benefits, summer savings expectations, travel allowances, and adjustments for use of outside scholarships.

(Manual at X-30-31) (emphasis added).

53. There were three main features of the Ivy Overlap process: all member institutions agreed to (1) award financial aid solely on the basis of applicants' demonstrated financial need, and not on the basis of academic or athletic ability; (2) jointly develop and apply a uniform needs analysis formula for assessing applicants' expected family contribution; and (3) jointly determine and apply

the family contribution determinations of commonly admitted students on a case-by-case basis.

54. The Ivy Overlap Group met approximately four times each year.

55. At the "Winter Meeting," usually held in New York City, the participants agreed upon the needs analysis methodology which the Ivy Overlap Group schools would employ in calculating family contribution for the next admitting class.

56. The participants attempted to establish the principles upon which need-assessment practices might be based and professional judgment might be exercised.

57. The agreed-upon principles of needs analysis were called the Ivy Needs Analysis Agreements. The Ivy methodology differed from the Congressional Methodology in significant respects.

58. The most meaningful departures from the Congressional Methodology concerned the apportionment of income when more than one child was attending college, the treatment of capital losses, depreciation losses, and losses from secondary businesses, and, in the case of divorced or separated parents, the treatment of assets of the noncustodial parent.

59. When more than one child in a family is attending college, the Congressional Methodology evenly apportions the parental contribution; for example, if two children in one family are attending college, half the parental contribution would be attributed to each child. By contrast, the Ivy methodology apportioned the family contribution for multiple siblings based on the cost of the colleges the children were attending. *294 The more a college cost,

the greater part of the family contribution would be attributed to the student attending that college.

60. The Congressional Methodology subtracts from income the losses reported on parents' tax returns. The Ivy Overlap Group schools did not subtract these losses in calculating income to determine family contribution.

61. In the event a student's parents were divorced or separated, the Congressional Methodology expects a contribution from the custodial parents only. The Ivy Overlap Group schools considered the income of the non-custodial parent.

62. MIT followed the Ivy Needs Analysis Agreements and used the Ivy methodology, with certain exceptions. These exceptions included the treatment of graduate student expenses, private schooling expenses, and certain student assets.

63. The Congressional Methodology expects that 6% of the parents' assets and 35% of the students' assets would be used for education. Apparently, upon the advice of financial planners, the parents of many aid applicants transfer most of the student's assets to the parents' accounts. MIT has observed that needy families do not avail themselves of this practice. With respect to needy families, if MIT finds than an inordinate amount of money is held in the student's name, it assigns a portion of this money to the parents' accounts. Further, unlike the other Ivy Overlap schools, MIT does not require a minimum parental contribution from certain very poor families.

64. At the annual "Spring Meeting," usually held in Wellesley, Massachusetts, the Ivy Overlap Group agreed upon the amount of the family contribution of commonly admitted aid applicants.

65. Prior to the Spring Meeting, financial aid officers at each school would personally review each financial aid application and determine independently the applicant's expected family contribution using the CSS family contribution determination, the Ivy methodology, and the school's professional judgment.

66. In preparation for the Spring Meeting, each institution compiled and then transmitted data concerning aid applicants to Student Aid Services, which is a private data processing company.

67. Student Aid Services used this data to prepare three separate "rosters."

68. The "master roster" comprised all aid applicants who had been admitted to an Ivy Overlap Group school.

69. The "bilateral roster" comprised those aid applicants who were admitted to two Ivy Overlap Group schools.

70. The "multilateral roster" comprised aid applicants who were admitted to three or more Ivy Overlap Group schools.

71. For each applicant, the rosters listed each school's student budget, proposed student and parent contribution, self-help levels, and grant awards.

72. The Spring Meeting lasted two days. The multilateral meetings were chaired by a "driver," who called out each applicant's name and the schools which had admitted that applicant. The schools would then compare their own separately calculated family

contribution figures with the other admitting schools' figures for that applicant.

73. More often than not, the family contribution determinations made by the various schools prior to the Spring Meeting were similar. The similarity resulted from the fact that, for the most part, each school used the identical needs analysis formula.

74. Family contribution differences of less than $500 were understood to be close enough not to warrant any discussion aimed at arriving at a common figure.

75. Where there were significant differences (in excess of $500), the schools would either agree upon a common figure or agree to meet somewhere at or near the middle of the divergent figures. Each institution adopted and used these agreed-upon family contribution determinations in making their financial aid awards, and expected the other institutions to do likewise.

*295 76. Due to time limitations at the Spring Meeting and the volume of cross-admitted students, the schools spent no more than a few minutes discussing divergent pre-meeting family contribution figures for individual students. During those few minutes allocated to individual aid applicants, the schools could not and did not make a genuine and concerted effort to assess accurately the aid applicant's actual financial circumstances, notwithstanding the expressed purpose of the Spring Meeting which was to utilize the combined expertise of the schools' financial aid staffs in order to arrive at the correct family contribution figure. The family contribution figures which were eventually agreed upon at the Spring Meeting were more a result of compromise and expediency than a genuine effort, as MIT contends, to "get it right."

77. As a result of the use of a common needs-analysis formula and the Spring Meeting, aid applicants and their families would pay the same amount regardless of which Ivy Overlap Group institution the student decided to attend.

78. Rarely did the participating schools fail to reach an agreement on the amount of the family contribution for individual students.

79. The Ivy Overlap Group schools also participated in a "post-overlap" process. The objective of the post-overlap process remained the same.

80. The post-overlap process involved students who "appealed" the family contribution determination that resulted from the Spring Meeting, students whose applications were incomplete at the time of the Spring Meeting, and students who were admitted from the wait list too late to be included in the Spring Meeting.

81. An Overlap II meeting was usually held to discuss aid applicants within the above categories who were admitted to three or more Ivy Overlap Group schools.

82. Aid applicants admitted to two Ivy Overlap Group schools were discussed by telephone or electronic "Bitnet" communication between the two schools.

83. The family contribution determinations, once agreed upon by the Ivy Overlap Group, remained in full force and effect until the student selected a school or a new agreement was reached between or among the affected schools.

84. Although the Ivy Overlap Group agreed upon the amount of the expected family contribution of aid applicants, the compo-

sition of individual aid packages was determined independently among the member institutions.

85. The Ivy Overlap Group also agreed not to provide merit aid to any applicant.

86. Merit aid is aid which is awarded on the basis of a student's personal virtues, such as academic achievement, athletic ability, musical talent, or past participation in extracurricular activities, irrespective of financial circumstances.

87. The Ivy Overlap Group awards aid solely on the basis of students' financial need. Students who have not demonstrated the need for financial assistance are not awarded aid.

88. Although witnesses on behalf of MIT testified at trial that the Ivy Overlap Group did not conceal its activities from the public or student-applicants and their families, the member schools made no effort to publicize the existence, purpose and effect of the Ivy Overlap Agreements.

89. For example, MIT's application brochure provided a step-by-step explanation of the financial aid application and award process. The brochure made no mention of the role which the Ivy Overlap Group played in that process even though Overlap is a standard and integral feature of the financial aid award process. Presumably, students admitted to more than one Ivy Overlap Group school were not aware that their expected family contribution was determined as a result of an arrangement by and between the Ivy Overlap Group schools.

90. The only other institution of higher education that provided the Ivy Overlap Group with any meaningful competition for

students was Stanford. The Ivy Overlap Group schools attempted to recruit Stanford into the group for fear that Stanford was luring high caliber students with merit scholarships and larger aid awards. Stanford refused the invitation upon its belief that Overlap violated the antitrust laws.

296 ENFORCEMENT OF OVERLAP

91. All Ivy Overlap Group schools recognized that a failure to comply with the Ivy Overlap Agreements could result in severe sanctions from the other institutions. Consequently, "cheating" was rare.

92. The few instances where an Ivy Overlap Group member violated the provisions of the Ivy Overlap Agreements provoked strong complaints from the other Ivy Overlap Group members.

93. In October 1986, Princeton began awarding $1,000 "research grants" to highly qualified undergraduates without regard to need. The other Ivy Overlap Group institutions viewed these awards as a form of merit scholarships which could entice students to attend Princeton and believed that the awards violated the spirit, if not the letter, of the Ivy Overlap Agreements. As a result of a series of complaints, Princeton agreed to abandon the awards.

III. DISCUSSION AND CONCLUSIONS OF LAW[1]
COMMERCE

MIT contends, as a threshold matter, that the Ivy Overlap Group is not susceptible to antitrust scrutiny because its activities did not constitute trade or commerce. Section 1 of the Sherman Act proscribes "[e]very contract, combination in the form of trust or otherwise, or conspiracy, in restraint of trade or commerce among the several states...." 15 U.S.C. § 1 (1990). It has become axiomatic that not every combination or conspiracy in restraint of trade or commerce is violative of the Sherman Act. For one thing, the Sherman Act, by its terms, only applies to contracts which restrain interstate trade or commerce.[2] Yet, not all conspiracies that affect interstate commerce are unlawful. The Supreme Court has noted that the Act was aimed at combinations and conspiracies which have commercial objectives and rarely is it applied to organizations or activities which are non-commercial in nature. *Klor's, Inc. v. Broadway-Hale Stores, Inc.,* 359 U.S. 207, 213 n. 7, 79 S.Ct. 705, 710 n. 7, 3 L.Ed.2d 741 (1959).

MIT endeavors to except the Overlap process from antitrust liability based on the assertion that it solely implicated non-commercial aspects of higher education. According to MIT, Overlap had a non-commercial impact, was not commercially motivated, *297 and was revenue neutral. MIT portrays Overlap's function as the "charitable" component of higher education, which was geared to advancing educational access and socio-economic diversity and maximizing the effective use of privately donated funds. MIT contends that Congress did not intend to subject the charitable functions of nonprofit entities to the proscriptions of the Sherman Act. [3]

MIT relies heavily on *Marjorie Webster Junior College v. Middle States Ass'n of Colleges and Secondary Schools,* 432 F.2d 650 (D.C.Cir.1970). The Middle States Association of Colleges and Secondary Schools, Inc. ("Middle States") is a nonprofit educational corporation which promotes quality in secondary schools and institutions of higher education in a particular geographical area. Chief among its functions is that of accrediting member institutions and those applying for membership. In 1966, Marjorie Webster Junior College, Inc., a proprietary junior college for women located in Washington, D.C., applied for membership with Middle States. Middle States refused the application because Marjorie Webster was not "a nonprofit organization with a governing board representing the public interest." Marjorie Webster brought suit to compel Middle States to consider its application for membership without regard to its proprietary character.

The District of Columbia Circuit Court of Appeals held that the activities of Middle States were non-commercial in nature and, as such, did not fall within the ambit of the Sherman Act. The court stated:

> [T]he proscriptions of the Sherman Act were "tailored * * * for the business world," not for the non-commercial aspects of the liberal arts and the learned professions. In these contexts, an incidental restraint on trade, absent an intent or purpose to affect the commercial aspects of the profession, is not sufficient to warrant application of the antitrust laws.

432 F.2d at 654 (footnotes omitted). The court went on to note the historical reluctance of Congress to exercise control in educational matters but added this disclaimer:

We need not suggest this reluctance [to control educational matters] is of such depth as to immunize any conceivable activity of appellant from regulation under the antitrust laws. It is possible to conceive of restrictions on eligibility for accreditation that could have little other than a commercial motive; and as such, antitrust policy would presumably be applied. Absent such motives, however, the process of accreditation is an activity distinct from the sphere of commerce; it goes rather to the heart of the concept of education itself.

432 F.2d at 654-55. This passage insinuates that the Sherman Act does not encompass restraints which operate in traditionally non-commercial domains, irrespective of their effects, unless the restraints were commercially motivated.[4] The Supreme Court rejected this "motivation" requirement and casted doubt on the breadth of *Marjorie Webster* in *Goldfarb v. Virginia State Bar,* 421 U.S. 773, 95 S.Ct. 2004, 44 L.Ed.2d 572 (1975).

In *Goldfarb,* the Court rejected defendant's attempt to carve out a learned profession exemption from the Sherman Act and held that a minimum fee schedule published by a county bar association and enforced by the Virginia State Bar violated § 1. The Court stated that "[t]he nature of an occupation, standing alone, does not provide sanctuary from the Sherman Act ... nor is the public-service aspect of professional practice controlling in determining whether § 1 includes professions." 421 *298 U.S. at 787, 95 S.Ct. at 2013. The Court explained that in drafting the Sherman Act, Congress intended to strike as broadly as it could. Thus, to recognize exceptions for entire categories of professions would conflict with Congress' intent.[5] Since *Goldfarb,* the Supreme Court has continually brought within the purview of the Sherman Act restraints involving traditionally "nonbusiness" areas. *See F.T.C. v. Indiana Fed'n of Dentists,* 476 U.S. 447, 106 S.Ct. 2009, 90 L.Ed.2d 445 (1986) (dental association's rules prohibiting members from submitting x-rays with claims forms); *National Collegiate*

Athletic Ass'n v. Board of Regents of the Univ. of Oklahoma, 468 U.S. 85, 104 S.Ct. 2948, 82 L.Ed.2d 70 (1984) (college athletic association's plan for televising college football games); *Hydrolevel, supra* (nonprofit trade association's promulgation of engineering standards); *National Soc. of Professional Engineers v. United States,* 435 U.S. 679, 98 S.Ct. 1355, 55 L.Ed.2d 637 (1978) (engineer society's canon of ethics prohibiting members from submitting competitive bids).

The court fails to see why the rationale of *Goldfarb* and its progeny with respect to learned professions should not apply with equal force to the field of education. The court does not mean to suggest that aspects of education which could have no conceivable commercial impact or effect would be subject to antitrust scrutiny. On the other hand, the court cannot ignore *Goldfarb's* admonition that profession-wide exemptions should be granted warily. Until the Supreme Court or Congress declare otherwise, the court will adhere to the rule that when an activity is commercial in nature, it falls under the aegis of the Sherman Act, regardless of the setting in which it takes place.

That MIT is a significant commercial entity is beyond peradventure. The magnitude of MIT's economic activity is certainly far greater than that of the vast majority of businesses. MIT has an operating budget of approximately $1.1 billion and an endowment of $1.5 billion. MIT's annual revenues from tuition, room and board charges are approximately $200 million.

MIT provides educational services to its students, for which they pay significant sums of money. The exchange of money for services is "'commerce' in the most common usage of that word." *Goldfarb,* 421 U.S. at 787-88, 95 S.Ct. at 2013. By agreeing upon aid applicants' families' expected financial contribution, the Ivy Overlap Group schools were setting the price aid applicants and their families would pay for educational services. The court can conceive of few aspects of higher education that are more commercial than the price charged to students.

MIT's attempt to disassociate the Overlap process from the commercial aspects of higher education is pure sophistry. Although MIT characterizes its financial aid as "charity," in essence, MIT provides a "discount" off the price of college offered to financial aid recipients. Further, accepting for the moment MIT's assertion that the impetus for instituting Overlap was to distribute more fairly limited financial resources for student aid, the means chosen to effectuate this goal, the elimination of merit scholarships and ensuring that commonly admitted aid recipients would pay the same regardless of which institution they decided to attend, is unquestionably commercial in nature. Not only did the effects of Overlap fall within the "sphere of commerce," but its existence struck at the heart of the commercial relationship between school and student.

PER SE v. RULE OF REASON

The language of the Sherman Act, taken literally, encompasses every conceivable contract or combination which affects commerce and is in restraint of trade. *Arizona v. Maricopa County Medical Soc.,* 457 U.S. 332, 342-43, 102 S.Ct. 2466, 2472, 73 L.Ed.2d 48 (1982). *See also Chicago Bd. of Trade v. United States,* 246 U.S. 231, 238, 38 S.Ct. 242, 244, 62 L.Ed. 683 (1918) ("Every agreement concerning trade, *299 every regulation of trade, restrains. To bind, to restrain, is of their very essence"); *United States v. Topco*

Assocs. Inc., 405 U.S. 596, 606, 92 S.Ct. 1126, 1133, 31 L.Ed.2d
515 (1972) ("Were § 1 to be read in the narrowest possible way,
any commercial contract could be deemed to violate it."). The
Supreme Court recognized that Congress could not have intended
a literal interpretation of the Act and concluded, drawing on its
legislative history, that only restraints which are "unreasonable" are
unlawful. *Standard Oil Co. v. United States,* 221 U.S. 1, 31 S.Ct.
502, 55 L.Ed. 619 (1911). Most types of restraints are judged by
the so-called "Rule of Reason." There are certain types of restraints,
however, which are by their nature so plainly anticompetitive and
are so lacking in redeeming virtue that they will be declared *per se*
unreasonable and conclusively presumed illegal without any further
analysis. *Broadcast Music Inc. v. Columbia Broadcasting Sys., Inc.,*
441 U.S. 1, 8, 99 S.Ct. 1551, 1556, 60 L.Ed.2d 1 (1979); *National
Soc. of Professional Engineers v. United States,* 435 U.S. 679, 692, 98
S.Ct. 1355, 1365, 55 L.Ed.2d 637 (1978); *Continental T.V., Inc.
v. GTE Sylvania, Inc.,* 433 U.S. 36, 50, 97 S.Ct. 2549, 2557, 53
L.Ed.2d 568 (1977); *Northern Pacific. Ry. Co. v. United States,* 356
U.S. 1, 5, 78 S.Ct. 514, 518, 2 L.Ed.2d 545 (1958). In *Northern
Pacific,* the Court explained the rationale behind the *per se* rules:

This principle of *per se* unreasonableness not only makes the
type of restraints which are proscribed by the Sherman Act more
certain to the benefit of everyone concerned, but it also avoids the
necessity for an incredibly complicated and prolonged economic
investigation into the entire history of the industry involved, as
well as related industries, in an effort to determine at large whether
a particular restraint has been unreasonable an inquiry so often
wholly fruitless when undertaken.

356 U.S. at 5, 78 S.Ct. at 518.

Horizontal agreements to fix prices have traditionally been subject to the *per se* rule. In *United States v. Socony-Vacuum Oil Co.,* 310 U.S. 150, 218-223, 60 S.Ct. 811, 842-44, 84 L.Ed. 1129 (1940), the Supreme Court reiterated the rule which is still in full force today:

> [F]or over forty years this Court has consistently and without deviation adhered to the principle that price-fixing agreements are unlawful per se under the Sherman Act. ...

> * * * * * *

Any combination which tampers with price structures is engaged in an unlawful activity. Even though the members of the price-fixing group were in no position to control the market, to the extent that they raised, lowered, or stabilized prices they would be directly interfering with the free play of market forces. The Act places all such schemes beyond the pale and protects any degree of interference. Congress has not left with us the determination of whether or not particular price-fixing schemes are wise or unwise, healthy or destructive.

Other types of restraints which the Supreme Court has declared as *per se* unreasonable include tying arrangements, *Jefferson Parish Hospital District No. 2 v. Hyde,* 466 U.S. 2, 104 S.Ct. 1551, 80 L.Ed.2d 2 (1984), vertical price fixing agreements, *United States v. Parke, Davis & Co.,* 362 U.S. 29, 80 S.Ct. 503, 4 L.Ed.2d 505 (1960), horizontal territory restrictions, *Topco Associates, supra,* and certain group boycotts, *United States v. General Motors Corp.,* 384

U.S. 127, 86 S.Ct. 1321, 16 L.Ed.2d 415 (1966); *Klor's, Inc. v. Broadway-Hale Stores, Inc.,* 359 U.S. 207, 79 S.Ct. 705, 3 L.Ed.2d 741 (1959).

Merely because a certain practice bears a label which falls within the categories of restraints declared to be *per se* unreasonable does not mean a court must reflexively condemn that practice to *per se* treatment. In *Broadcast Music,* the Supreme Court refused to apply the *per se* rule to a system whereby licensing agencies for composers, writers and publishers received fees for the issuance of blanket licenses to *300 perform copyrighted musical compositions.[6] The Court reasoned that not every agreement which may be characterized as price fixing in the literal sense is the type of restraint to which the *per se* rule is meant to apply. The Court stated:

> As generally used in the antitrust field, "price fixing" is a shorthand way of describing certain categories of business behavior to which the *per se* rule has been held applicable. The Court of Appeal's literal approach does not alone establish that this particular practice is one of those types or that it is "plainly anti-competitive" and very likely without "redeeming virtue." Literalness is overly simplistic and often overbroad. When two partners set the price of their goods or services they are literally "price fixing," but they are not *per se* in violation of the Sherman Act.... Thus, it is necessary to characterize the challenged conduct as falling within or without that category of behavior to which we

apply the label *"per se* price fixing." That will often,
but not always, be a simple matter.

441 U.S. at 10, 99 S.Ct. at 1557 (citations omitted). *See e.g.*
National Collegiate Athletic Ass'n v. Board of Regents of the Univ. of
Oklahoma, 468 U.S. 85, 104 S.Ct. 2948, 82 L.Ed.2d 70 (1984)
(inappropriate to apply *per se* rule because horizontal restraints on
competition are essential if product is to be available at all).

In *Goldfarb*, the Supreme Court cautioned against applying
rigid, inflexible rules to restraints which occupy "non-business" set-
tings. The Court characterized as price fixing a state bar minimum
fee schedule for legal services but nonetheless scrutinized the practice under the Rule of Reason. In what since has become a widely
discussed footnote, the Court remarked:

The fact that a restraint operates upon a profession as distinguished from a business is, of course, relevant in determining
whether that particular restraint violates the Sherman Act. It would
be unrealistic to view the practice of professions as interchangeable
with other business activities, and automatically to apply to the
professions antitrust concepts which originated in other areas. The
public service aspect, and other features of the professions, may
require that a particular practice, which could properly be viewed
as a violation of the Sherman Act in another context, be treated
differently.

421 U.S. at 788 n. 17; 95 S.Ct. at 2013. *See also Professional*
Engineers, supra.

As the above cited footnote from *Goldfarb* and later Supreme
Court holdings make clear, courts should extend hesitantly
the reaches of the *per se* rule to nonbusiness contexts so that at

least some attempt is made to see whether the way in which the restraint acts upon a profession's particular characteristics has economic effects which would warrant special consideration under the Sherman Act.

In *Arizona v. Maricopa County Medical Soc.,* 457 U.S. 332, 102 S.Ct. 2466, 73 L.Ed.2d 48 (1982), the Court applied the *per se* rule in invalidating a maximum fee schedule for medical services. Nevertheless, the Court signaled that it was not retreating from the rationale of *Goldfarb:*

The price-fixing agreements in this case, however, are not premised on public service or ethical norms. The respondents do not argue, as did the defendants in *Goldfarb* and *Professional Engineers,* that the quality of the professional service that their members provide is enhanced by the price restraints.

Id., 457 at 349, 102 S.Ct. at 2475. The Court stressed that *per se* invalidation was proper since the effects of the maximum price schedule did not distinguish the medical profession from any other provider of goods and services. The policy of applying reluctantly *per se* rules to the learned professions was reaffirmed just a few years later. In *FTC v. Indiana Fed'n of Dentists,* 476 U.S. 447, 106 S.Ct. 2009, 90 *301 L.Ed.2d 445 (1986), the Federal Trade Commission challenged a dental association regulation which forbid members to submit x-rays to dental insurers in conjunction with claims requests. The Court declined to apply the *per se* rule on the basis that:

[W]e have been slow to condemn rules adopted by professional associations as unreasonable *per se* ... and, in general, to extend *per se* analysis to restraints imposed in the context of business relationships where the economic impact of certain practices is not immediately obvious.

Id., 476 U.S. at 459-460, 106 S.Ct. at 2018 (citations omitted). The court's decision to apply the Rule of Reason does not stem from a reluctance to characterize the Ivy Overlap process as the type of price fixing which is ordinarily *per se* unreasonable.[7] These activities amount to more than price fixing in the literal sense. The Ivy Overlap Group members, which are horizontal competitors, agreed upon the price which aid applicants and their families would have to pay to attend a member institution to which that student had been accepted. Further, the Ivy Overlap Group's agreed-upon ban on merit scholarships foreclosed the possibility that non-aid applicants could receive a discount based on any type of meritorious achievement. *See Catalano, Inc. v. Target Sales, Inc.,* 446 U.S. 643, 648, 100 S.Ct. 1925, 1928, 64 L.Ed.2d 580 (1980) ("[A]n agreement to eliminate discounts ... falls squarely within the traditional *per se* rules against price fixing."). Nevertheless, in the exercise of caution and in light of the Supreme Court's repeated counsel against presumptive invalidation of restraints involving professional associations, the court will scrutinize the Ivy Overlap Group under the Rule of Reason.

RULE OF REASON

Application of the Rule of Reason has changed very little since Justice Brandeis' explanation in *Chicago Bd. of Trade v. United States,* 246 U.S. 231, 238, 38 S.Ct. 242, 244, 62 L.Ed. 683 (1918):

The true test of legality is whether the restraint is such as merely regulates and perhaps thereby promotes competition or whether it is such as may suppress or even destroy competition. To determine that question the court must ordinarily consider the facts peculiar to the business to which the restraint is applied; its condition before and after the restraint was imposed; the nature of the restraint and its effect, actual or probable. The history of the restraint, the evil believed to exist, the reason for adopting the particular remedy, the purpose or end sought to be attained, are all relevant facts.

In *National Soc. of Professional Engineers v. United States,* 435 U.S. 679, 689, 98 S.Ct. 1355, 1365, 55 L.Ed.2d 637 (1978), however, the Court emphasized that the Rule of Reason "does not open the field of antitrust inquiry to any argument in favor of a challenged restraint that may fall within the realm of reason." The proper inquiry is limited to whether the restraint in question "is one that promotes competition or one that suppresses competition." *Id.,* 435 U.S. at 692, 98 S.Ct. at 1365.

The evidence adduced at trial clearly established that the awarding of financial incentives in the form of aid by institutions of higher education is a traditional feature of student recruitment. The evidence also established that the receipt of financial incentives in the form of aid weighs heavily in a student's and his or her family's decision-making process with respect to which *302 school to attend.[8] No reasonable person could conclude that the Ivy Overlap Agreements did not suppress competition. As a result of the Ivy Overlap Agreements, the member schools created a horizontal restraint which interfered with the natural functioning of the marketplace by eliminating students' ability to consider price differences when choosing a school and by depriving students of the ability to receive financial incentives which competition between those schools may have generated. Indeed, the member institutions formed the Ivy Overlap Group for the very purpose of eliminating economic competition for students. One need look no further than the language of the Agreements themselves, which directly proclaimed the intent to neutralize the effect of financial aid so that a student may choose among Ivy Group institutions for reasons other than cost.

In addition to the express commands of the Ivy Overlap Agreements, there was abundant and uncontroverted evidence that the fundamental objective of the Ivy Overlap Group was to eliminate price competition among the member institutions. Pursuant to this end, the schools devised a common methodology of needs analysis, exchanged prospective self-help tuition and other budgetary information, agreed not to award merit scholarships and compared and adjusted proposed family contributions at annual Spring Meetings. Each of these elements served to ensure that families would pay approximately the same amount regardless of the Ivy Group institution the student chose to attend. Consequently, since the school would not compete financially for students, the awarding of aid was unresponsive to the demands of students and their families. These agreements were enforced, cheating was rare, and the schools even attempted to recruit Stanford, the only other school which provided any meaningful competition for the same student base, to participate in the process.

The actual economic repercussions of the Ivy Overlap Agreements was the subject of much focus at trial. The government and MIT attempted to demonstrate, both empirically and theoretically, the effect that Overlap had on the price of education at the Ivy Overlap Group schools.[9] Whether or *303 not Overlap increased or decreased net revenues, to the extent it is even capable of being proved with a reasonable degree of economic certainty, is, nevertheless, not germane to the resolution of this case, nor is the array of studies and comparisons the government submitted purporting to demonstrate other tangible anticompetitive effects of Overlap.[10] The economists' theoretical models and empirical analyses, while quite interesting, do no more than distract the court from the inescapable truth that by entering into the Ivy Overlap Agreements, the member institutions purposefully removed, by agreement, price considerations and price competition for an Overlap school education.

The Rule of Reason ordinarily requires an in-depth inquiry into the actual market impact of a restraint. There are some agreements, however, that are so inherently suspect, that even under the Rule of Reason "no elaborate industry analysis is required to demonstrate [their] anticompetitive character." *FTC v. Indiana Fed'n of Dentists,* 476 U.S. 447, 459, 106 S.Ct. 2009, 2018, 90 L.Ed.2d 445 (1986); *Professional Engineers,* 435 U.S. at 692, 98 S.Ct. at 1366. This is such an agreement. By agreeing among themselves not to offer merit scholarships, the Ivy Overlap schools in effect agreed not to compete for students by using competitive discounts based on merit, which deprived students, needy or not, of the opportunity to receive competitive *304 tuition reductions. By ensuring that students and their families would pay the same amount regardless of which Ivy Overlap Group institution the student decided to attend, whether it was a result of the common-needs analysis formula or by actual discussions at the Spring Meeting or the post-Overlap process, the Ivy Overlap Agreements denied students the ability to compare prices when choosing among the Ivy Overlap Group institutions. A market which is unresponsive to consumer preference infringes upon the most fundamental principle of anti-trust law. In fact, MIT's defense, that competition for students would lead to the erosion of need-blind admissions and need-based aid, "confirms, rather than refutes the anticompetitive purpose and effect of its agreement." *Professional Engineers,* 435 U.S. at 693, 98 S.Ct. at 1366.

No showing that Overlap did not result in more profits for the colluding schools can camouflage its effect on competition. To suggest otherwise would be to greatly misperceive the ills which the Sherman Act was intended to cure. The Sherman Act presumes that any tampering with the free forces of the market is detrimental. Consequently, any agreement that interferes with the setting of price in the free market "is illegal on its face." *Id.,* 435 U.S. at 692, 98 S.Ct. at 1365. MIT may argue that competition was not harmed because the Ivy Overlap process did not raise price, but as far as the Sherman Act is concerned, when competition is eliminated, competition is harmed. As the Supreme Court stated in *Indiana Federation of Dentists:*

A refusal to compete with respect to the package of services offered to customers, no less than a refusal to compete with respect to the price term of an agreement, impairs the ability of the market to advance social welfare by ensuring the provision of desired goods and services to consumers at a price approximating the marginal cost of providing them. Absent some countervailing procompetitive virtue such as, for example, the creation of efficiencies in the operation of a market or the provision of goods and services ... such an agreement limiting consumer choice by impeding the "ordinary give and take of the market place," ... cannot be sustained under the Rule of Reason.

476 U.S. at 459, 106 S.Ct. at 2018 (citations omitted).

Since the Ivy Overlap Agreements are plainly anticompetitive, the Rule of Reason places upon MIT "a heavy burden of establishing an affirmative defense which competitively justifies this apparent deviation from the operations of a free market." *National Collegiate Athletic Ass'n v. Board of Regents of the Univ. of Oklahoma*, 468 U.S. 85, 113, 104 S.Ct. 2948, 2966, 82 L.Ed.2d 70 (1984). Even accepting MIT's premise that Overlap was revenue neutral, to say that a restraint is revenue neutral, by itself, says nothing of its procompetitive virtue.

MIT offers the following justifications. MIT contends that Overlap actually enhanced competition in that it provided opportunities for needy students who otherwise would not have been able to attend the Ivy Overlap Group institutions, without limiting the choices available to non-needy students who did not require financial assistance. MIT also professes that Overlap enhanced competition among students for limited enrollment opportunities and competition among the member schools in areas such as the curriculum, campus life, vocational opportunities and reputation. MIT's principal defense is that only by coordinating several aspects of their financial aid programs are the Ivy Overlap Group schools able to assure that students are admitted only on the basis of merit and that the full financial need of admitted students is met. According to MIT, the Ivy Overlap Group schools' administrators and financial aid officers are under constant pressure from faculty, alumni and others to enroll the most qualified student body possible. MIT insists that without Overlap's obligations and disciplines, the member institutions will presumably, one by one, succumb to these pressures to attract the most desirable students, and, eventually, engage in a bidding war for the "best of the brightest" by offering merit scholarships *305 and increased grant awards. As a consequence, the schools will find it necessary to shift "limited" financial aid resources to highly qualified but non-needy students, which in turn will significantly decrease the availability of need-based aid. MIT, echoing the sentiments of other Ivy Overlap Group institutions, explained that it "could not idly sit by and watch significant numbers of the best and brightest students attend other institutions due to large scholarship awards ... [F]aced with this situation, MIT would be forced to respond." MIT's Post-Trial Memorandum at 38.

The effects of the elimination of need-blind admissions and need-based aid, according to MIT, would be devastating. It would undermine efforts to maintain educational access and opportunity and impede socio-economic diversity, which would lessen the over-all quality of education. These policies, according to MIT, have dramatically changed the character of American education:

> These programs have enabled large numbers of needy students to obtain a high quality college edu-cation despite their inability to pay for it. Minority groups, which are disproportionately represented among the class of high need students, have experienced greatly improved educational access. Providing educational opportunity to these stu-dents benefits the individual student by providing him or her with the skills to compete and succeed in the labor market, benefits society by increasing the education level of its members and enhancing

the ranks of productive, tax-paying citizens, and provides hope to similarly situated students who see their predecessors succeed. It also improves the educational experience of classmates of needy students, who are exposed to a greater diversity of viewpoints and ideas.

MIT's Post-Trial Memorandum at 5.

The issue before the court is not, as MIT suggests, whether the Sherman Act permits institutions of higher education to maintain the policies of need-blind admissions and need-based aid. Every institution, with or without Overlap, is free to embrace independently any admission and financial aid policy it wishes, and most do. The court is not to decide whether social policy aims can ever justify an otherwise competitively unreasonable restraint. The issue before the court is narrow, straightforward and unvarnished. It is whether, under the Rule of Reason, the elimination of competition itself can be justified by non-economic designs. The Supreme Court has unambiguously and conclusively held that it may not.

In *Professional Engineers*, the Supreme Court nullified an engineering association's canon of ethics prohibiting its members from engaging in competitive bidding for engineering services. The association contended that the ban on competition was justified because without it, engineers would be pressured to design and manufacture structures and offer other engineering services at the lowest possible price, which would lead to inferior work and, in turn, pose a danger to public safety, health and welfare. The Supreme Court stated that it has never accepted such an argument. Whatever the risk that competition may lead to inferior engineering services, the basic policy underlying the Sherman Act "precludes inquiry into the question whether competition is good or bad." *Professional Engineers,* 435 U.S. at 695, 98 S.Ct. at 1367. The court stated that:

Petitioner's ban on competitive bidding prevents all customers from making price comparisons in the initial selection of an engineer, and imposes the Society's views of the costs and benefits of competition on the entire marketplace. It is this restraint that must be justified under the Rule of Reason, and Petitioner's attempt to do so on the basis of the potential threat that competition poses to the public safety and the ethics of its profession is nothing more than a frontal assault on the basic policy of the Sherman Act.

Id., 435 U.S. at 695, 98 S.Ct. at 1367.

The Supreme Court reaffirmed these principles in *Indiana Federation of Dentists,* wherein an association of dentists ***306** challenged a Federal Trade Commission determination that a conspiracy among Indiana dentists to refuse to comply with requests by dental insurers to submit x-rays for use claims determinations was an unreasonable restraint of trade in violation of § 1 of the Sherman Act and, consequently violated § 5 of the Federal Trade Communications Act. The dental insurers requested the x-rays pursuant to newly developed "alternative benefits plans," which were cost containment measures requiring insurers to evaluate dentists' diagnoses and recommendations so as to ensure that dentists provide the patient with the "least expensive yet adequate treatment." Among the association's defenses which the Supreme Court rejected was the so-called "quality of care defense." The dentists argued that x-rays, in and of themselves, are not sufficient bases for diagnosis and treatment determination. They added that if insurers ground their claims decisions solely on an examination of x-rays to the exclusion of other diagnostic aids available to dentists, then the risk exists that insurers may improperly refuse to pay for treatment that is in the best interest of the patient. In dismissing such justifications, the Court again characterized as an affront to the Sherman Act the belief that in an unrestrained market wherein consumers are given access to information they believe is relevant to their choices, consumers will be led into making unwise and dangerous choices. The Court stated:

The premise of the argument is that, far from having no effect on the cost of dental services chosen by patients and their insurers, the provision of x-rays will have too great an impact: it will lead to the reduction of costs through the selection of inadequate treatment. Precisely such a justification for withholding information from customers was rejected as illegitimate in [*Professional Engineers*].

FTC, 476 U.S. at 463, 106 S.Ct. at 2020.

MIT's defense is indistinguishable from the defenses offered in *Professional Engineers* and *Indiana Federation of Dentists*. The Ivy Overlap Group believes that only by eliminating competition is it able to ensure that scarce financial resources are allocated in a manner which it deems to be most advantageous. In so doing, the Ivy Overlap Group was simply imposing its view of the costs and benefits of competition on the marketplace for an education at the elite institutions of higher education.

The ways in which our nation profits when our many great institutions of higher education open their doors to those who for too long were denied the privilege of attending college are immeasurable. These policies send an important signal to a large segment of our society that persons need not presume they are unable to attend college for fear of not being able to afford what has become the extraordinary cost of higher education. Nor can it be denied, as the testimony of several witnesses attested, that cultural and economic diversity contributes to the quality of education and enhances the vitality of campus life. What can be questioned, however, is whether the scheme whereby the Ivy Overlap Group schools conspire to remove price as a facet of competition for students is a necessary ingredient to achieve these ends.

The court is unconvinced because there is no evidence supporting MIT's fatalistic prediction that the end of the Ivy Overlap Group necessarily would sound the death knell of need-blind admissions or need-based aid. MIT has relentlessly emphasized, at each stage of this case, the benefits fostered by the policies of need-blind admissions and need-based aid. Almost every witness testifying on MIT's behalf spoke of how the institutions themselves benefitted from a culturally and economically diverse student body. Yet, the message to be gleaned from MIT's defense is that the moment the Ivy Overlap Group schools are no longer able to jointly eliminate price competition, they will immediately bow to faculty pressure to enroll the very highest caliber student at high cost and at the expense of needy students, leaving behind hallowed principles of equality of educational access and opportunity and the resultant societal benefits which they have so ardently underscored. William Bowen, past President of Princeton University, *307 believes that if Overlap ends, the member schools will take "one step back toward the economic segregation of higher education." Can the Ivy Overlap Group members' purposes be so fragile that their primary goal of having the most desirable students outweighs their ability, without Overlap, to pursue diligently even an imperfect policy of promoting the virtue of student diversity and the advantages of making available to needy students the benefits of these elite educational institutions? Will there also be lost the value to be gained by signaling to all prospective students that they can in fact aspire to attend an Ivy Overlap Group institution even though their families may be of limited means? The court thinks not. If MIT and the other Ivy League schools were to so easily abandon these objectives merely because Overlap was not in play, then the court could only conclude that their professed dedication to these ends was less than sincere.

By the same token, if these policies are as meaningful as MIT avows, and these institutions refuse in any way to forsake admitting the "best of the best," then they should be willing to dedicate the necessary resources to ensure the continuation of these policies. It is certainly true that these decisions, like nearly every important decision these schools must make, will be difficult and will have a financial impact in other areas of the schools' operations. The end of Overlap will only portend the end of need-blind admissions and schools' ability to guarantee the full need of their aid applicants if the schools decide that other financial priorities occupy a higher investment and financial plane. The dilemma over resource allocation always triggers budgetary balancing, and that is likely to be called for here. Such balancing is not new, nor is it unreasonable, if the suggested method of avoiding it is to act contrary to the law.

Lastly, MIT urges the court to assess the Ivy Overlap Group against the background of our national education policy, the cornerstone of which, for several decades, has been the advancement of equality of educational access and opportunity. The allure of approaching this case in such a posture is evident. The court, is obligated, however, to judge Overlap against a different framework: that of the Sherman Act, which, though not as old as MIT, has nevertheless for more than a century guided our Nation's economic policies. MIT insists that Overlap must be sustained because "leaving educational opportunity to the vagaries of the commercial marketplace would hurt society and be unfair to individuals." MIT's Post-Trial Memorandum at 2. Congress, in passing the Sherman Act, made a very different value judgment, that far from hurting society and the individual, an unrestrained and unencumbered marketplace is their best protector:

The Sherman Act was designed to be a comprehensive charter of economic liberty aimed at preserving free and unfettered competition as the rule of trade. It rests on the premise that the unrestrained interaction of competitive forces will yield the best allocation of our economic resources, the lowest prices, the highest quality and the greatest material progress, while at the same time providing an environment conducive to the preservation of our democratic political and social institutions.

Northern Pacific Ry Co. v. United States, 356 U.S. 1, 4, 78 S.Ct. 514, 517, 2 L.Ed.2d 545 (1958). Congress is certainly free to decide that our national education policy could be better served by Overlap than by the operation of an unfettered marketplace. Until Congress declares otherwise, however, the court has no choice but to respect 102 years of our nation's antitrust policy.

NOTES

[1] Soon after the trial was completed Congress passed the Higher Education Amendments of 1992. Pub.L. No. 102-325, 106 Stat. 448 (1992). Section 1544 of the Amendments makes lawful, for

a two year period, certain Ivy Overlap Group activity which is the subject of this civil action. Section 1544 states in its entirety:

(a) Effect on Pending Cases Prohibited. Nothing in this section shall in any way be construed to affect any antitrust litigation pending on the date of enactment of this Act.

(b) In General. Except as provided in subsections (a), (c), and (e), institutions of higher education may

(1) voluntarily agree with any other institution of higher education to award financial aid not awarded under the Higher Education Act of 1965 to students attending those institutions only on the basis of demonstrated financial need for such aid; and

(2) discuss and voluntarily adopt defined principles of professional judgment for determining student financial need for aid not awarded under the Higher Education Act of 1965.

(c) Exception. Institutions of higher education shall not discuss or agree with each other on the prospective financial aid award to a specific common applicant for financial aid.

(d) Related Matter. No inference of unlawful contract, combination, or conspiracy shall be drawn from the fact that institutions of higher education engage in conduct authorized by this section.

(e) Sunset provision. This section shall expire on September 30, 1994.

Due to the Effect on Pending Cases Prohibition clause and the fact that the statute is limited in duration, the court will issue its opinion without regard to these provisions.

[2] The existence of interstate commerce is both a jurisdictional requirement and an element of the substantive offense. *Cardio-Medical Assoc., Ltd. v. Crozer-Chester Medical Center,* 721 F.2d 68, 71 (3d Cir. 1983). MIT concedes that the activities challenged in this case are sufficiently interstate in nature. MIT sends brochures and applications to prospective students in every state and admits many non-Massachusetts residents. In addition, MIT receives charitable contributions from individuals and corporations from around the country. Accordingly, the court will not address this issue.

[3] MIT's status as a nonprofit corporation, on its own, does not shield its conduct from the Sherman Act. *See American Soc'y of Mechanical Engineers, Inc. v. Hydrolevel Corp.,* 456 U.S. 556, 577, 102 S.Ct. 1935, 1948, 72 L.Ed.2d 330 (1982) ("[I]t is beyond debate that nonprofit organizations can be held liable under the antitrust laws.").

[4] Presumably, however, under *Marjorie Webster,* once a court finds that such a restraint was commercially motivated, the court would examine the restraint's reasonableness and effects, irrespective of motivation. *See Association for Intercollegiate Athletics for Women v. National Collegiate Athletic Ass'n,* 735 F.2d 577, 583 n. 6 (D.C.Cir.1984).

[5] The Court did specify, however, that distinctions between businesses and professions are meaningful in other contexts, particularly when evaluating whether a particular restraint is lawful. *See* discussion of *Goldfarb, infra.*

[6] The court held that the establishment of a price for the blanket licenses was an incidental, albeit necessary, consequence of the creation of the licenses themselves. Further, the licensing system did not place any restraints on the ability of copyright owners to sell their compositions.

[7] The court's refusal to adopt a *per se* approach is not based, as MIT urges, upon the lack of experience among courts with regard to Overlap agreements. *See Topco Associates,* 405 U.S. at 607-08, 92 S.Ct. at 1133 ("It is only after considerable experience with certain business relationships that courts classify them as *per se* violations of the Sherman Act"). As the Supreme Court commented in *Maricopa,* 457 U.S. at 349 n. 19, 102 S.Ct. at 2475, this argument confuses "the established position that a *new per se* rule is not justified until the judiciary obtains considerable rule-of-reason experience with the particular type of restraint challenged." (italics in original; underline added). The challenged conduct in the present case involves price fixing, which is hardly a new type of restraint.

[8] An educational counselor for MIT succinctly explained the relationship between costs and the college selection process:

> [Students] are always concerned about money. They are always concerned about money. They are typically concerned less about whether the curriculum is right for them or not. That's sort of a sec-

ond tier kind of a thinking, people don't get to that while they are applying a lot of times.

(N.T. 1515).

[9] MIT contends that while economic theory can predict the behavior of a for-profit firm, since by definition its primary motivation is profitmaximization, economic theory cannot predict the consequences of cooperative behavior among non-profit institutions such as colleges, since non-profit educational institutions have diverse interests, some of which may conflict with the goal of profit-maximization. MIT contends that basic economic theory rejects a presumption that bona fide non-profit organizations that act cooperatively will do so in a way that harms the consumer.

The government's expert economist, on the other hand, testified that institutions of higher education are motivated to collude, just as profitmaximizers are. According to the government's economist, colleges compete for many things such as students, faculty, and financial support. By minimizing the competition for students, the schools can increase their revenue as compared to costs. Since these institutions do not distribute profit among owners, the decision-makers can consume these increases in other ways, such as greater travel funds, higher faculty salaries, improved facilities, etc. According to the government's economist, the only distinction between for-profit and non-profit entities is the way in which they consume profit for-profit entities distribute profits among the owners, while non-profit entities distribute profits within the organization. This distinction, concludes the government's expert, has no significance economically.

Both the government and MIT set out to substantiate their theories and demonstrate empirically what each believed to be the proper relationship between Ivy Overlap Agreements and the price of an Overlap institution education, or, phrased differently, whether the price for an education rose as a result of Overlap. Both experts agreed that price is properly defined as average net revenue per student, but the similarity in approaches ended there. The government's economist chose to compare the average net revenue per student of the Ivy Overlap Group schools with the average net revenue per student of several different schools which he deemed to be comparable. MIT's expert conducted a multiple regression analysis, a method which permits an economist to isolate a single variable in a multiple-variable environment. Only by controlling for numerous factors which could have an effect on net price, according to MIT's economist, is it possible to gauge accurately Overlap's effect on net price. To that end, his study compared over 220 institutions with available data. Not surprisingly, each economist arrived at very different conclusions. The government's comparisons showed that the average net revenue per student for the Ivy Overlap schools was generally higher than the average net revenue per student for other comparable schools. The difference, according to the government's expert, was economically significant and demonstrated that the Overlap process had an effect of raising the average net revenues of the Ivy Overlap Group schools. MIT's regression analysis, on the other hand, revealed no demonstrable statistical effect of Overlap on average net price per student. MIT's expert concluded, as a result, that the Ivy Overlap schools did not take in more revenue as a result of Overlap, as it would have in Overlap's absence.

[10] The government presented an array of studies and comparisons purporting to demonstrate tangible anticompetitive effects of Overlap. The government points out that the Ivy Needs Methodology taxes a larger amount of income and assets for the family contribution determination than does the Congressional Methodology. The effect of this, according to the government's economist, is that the agreed-upon financial contributions was greater than it would have been had the Ivy Needs Methodology not been employed. The government also presented comparisons showing that the needy and minorities, the two groups MIT asserts are the direct beneficiaries of Overlap, had higher family contributions as a result of Overlap as well.

Further, the government demonstrated how the Spring Meeting negatively affected the economic opportunities available to students. The government's economist examined the bilateral rosters that MIT had with each of the Ivy League schools for 1988, paying special attention to handwritten changes that were made to the family contribution figures at the Spring Meeting, to the extent the changes were decipherable. He then compared the average family contribution of all the schools before changes were made with the average family contribution of all schools after changes were made. This comparison revealed that the changes made at the bilateral meeting did not result in a economically significant increase to the schools' average family contribution. This did not mean that there was not a significant impact on the price paid by students and their families, however. To demonstrate, the government's economist posed the following hypothetical: Before the Spring Meeting, student x had a family contribution, as calculated by MIT, of $2,000, and a family contribution, as calculated by Harvard, of $6,000.

At the bilateral meeting, MIT and Harvard met in the middle and agreed that student x's family contribution would be $4,000. This would obviously mean that MIT's family contribution is up, Harvard's is down, and as to the average for the two schools, there has been no change. From the perspective of student x and his or her family, however, their "best financial opportunity" has increased by $2,000. The government's economist defined "best financial opportunity" as the difference between the lowest price that family faced before the reconciliation and that which it faced after the reconciliation. He found that on average, the "best financial opportunity" for those students whose family contribution was changed at the 1988 bilateral meetings increased by $1,091, a figure which he deemed to be economically significant.

MIT assailed the accuracy of the government's data and challenged the significance of the conclusions that the government sought the court to draw from this evidence. Much of MIT's criticism was sound.

 **Department of Justice**

FOR IMMEDIATE RELEASE
WEDNESDAY, DECEMBER 22, 1993

AT
(202) 616-2771

JUSTICE DEPARTMENT SETTLES
MIT PRICE FIXING CASE

WASHINGTON, D.C. — The Department of Justice's Antitrust Division announced today that the Massachusetts Institute of Technology (MIT) has accepted its offer to settle a case in which the university was charged with fixing the prices financial aid applicants paid to attend college.

"Throughout this entire case, the Department has had one goal in mind — to protect the interests of all students and their families in obtaining an affordable college education. This settlement reaches that goal," said Robert E. Litan, Deputy Assitant Attorney General for the Antitrust Division.

"The Justice Department continues to believe "Overlap" is illegal and violates the antitrust laws. This settlement will not restore "Overlap"," Litan added.

"Overlap" was the name given to the collusive practice by which MIT and the Ivy League colleges met each Spring to agree on how much money a particular student and his family would have to pay to attend a member school.

Under today's settlement, MIT acknowledges that it is obliged in its dealings with the Ivy League colleges to act in accordance with a 1991 consent decree in which Brown, Columbia, Cornell, Dartmough, Harvard, Princeton, the University of Pennsylvania, and Yale agreed not to fix tuition, faculty salaries, or the payments needy students would be expected to make on their own.

MIT has further promised that in its dealings with other schools it will abide by standards of conduct, agreed upon today, that prohibit any discussion or agreement on the contribution expected to be made by students receiving financial aid. The standards also prohibit any discussion or agreement on the composition of financial aid packages.

The settlement further prohibits MIT from conspiring with other colleges to fix tuition figures and faculty salaries.

Said Litan, "The evidence at trial showed that MIT exchanged proposed tuition levels with the Ivy League colleges, and then used the prices the Ivies intended to charge in setting its own tuition. The settlement prohibits that kind of activity."

Under today's settlement, MIT may agree with other colleges on general principles for determining financial aid, to award aid solely on the basis of financial need, and to exchange limited data about applicants' financial profiles.

In order to do this, MIT and any other participating schools must commit to need-blind admissions and to meet the full financial need of their undergraduate students.

"This commitment ensures that students will not lose the opportunity to attend MIT or other participating colleges because they or their families cannot afford to pay," Litan said.

After a 1992 trial, the U.S. District Court ruled that MIT had violated the price fixing laws. The Court of Appeals sent the case back for further analysis.

"The Court of Appeals remanded this case because of very unique issues associated with awarding financial aid to students. That opinion and this settlement will have no effect on how the Department views other activities and businesses—whether they are for-profit or non-profit," said Litan.

###

93-406

(NOTE: This is a reproduction of the Department of Justice press release dated December 23, 1993 made to aid legibility. Copies of the actual press release are available from the Department of Justice.)

APPENDIX C

(NOTE: This reproduction of the actual letter was made to aid legibility. Copies of the actual letter are available from the Department of Justice.)

PALMER & DODGE
One Beacon Street
Boston, Massachusetts 02106

Thane D. Scott, Esq.
(617) 573-0154

Telephone: (617) 573-0160
Facsimile: (617) 227-4420

December 22, 1993

VIA FACSIMILE AND OVERNIGHT COURIER

Robert E. Litan, Esq.
Deputy Assistant Attorney General
Antitrust Division
United States Department of Justice
Room 3208, 10th & Constitution Ave., N.W.
Washington, D.C. 20503

Re: U.S. v. Brown University, et al.

Dear Mr. Litan:

I am writing on behalf of the Massachusetts Institute of Technology ("MIT"), which has authorized me to make the following representations regarding United States v. Brown University, et al., No. 91-CV-3274 (E.D. pa.). MIT acknowledges that Federal Rule of Civil Procedure 65(d) precludes it from acting in concert with any of the Ivy League colleges in a manner that violates the Final Judgment entered on September 19, 1991 in United States v. Brown University, et al. ("Consent Decree"). If MIT does so, it may be subject to contempt sanctions unless the conduct falls within Section IX of the Consent Decree ("Limiting Conditions") or a subsequent modification of the Consent Decree.

Schools participating with MIT in cooperative financial aid arrangements may rely upon the attached document ("Standards of Conduct") as setting forth standards agreeable to the United States. Upon reasonable request, MIT will provide the United States with non-privileged documents, including reports received from the independent third party referenced in the Standards of Conduct, and other information reasonably related to MIT's participation in the conduct described in the attached document. Upon annual written request, MIT shall inform the United States in writing (a) whether in the preceding year MIT has participated in conduct of the type described in the attached document and, if so, (b) whether such conduct was consistent with the Standards of Conduct.

Upon the request of any Ivy League college, the United States and that college shall jointly move for and support modification of the Consent Decree to incorporate the standards set forth in the attached document. As MIT has agreed to observe the terms of the Standards of Conduct in its interactions with other institutions, the parties will execute a stipulation of dismissal under Rule 41(a) and the United States will move to dismiss the pending case against MIT. MIT understands that the Justice Department is amenable to this resolution because of the special procedural posture of this case and the Third Circuit's holding that unique standards apply to the awarding of financial aid by colleges.

Very truly yours,

Thane D. Scott

TDS:cas
Enclosure

STANDARDS OF CONDUCT

1. Non-profit institutions of higher education may participate in the cooperative financial aid arrangements set forth below ("Participating Schools"), provided that they:

   a) practice need-blind admissions; that is, admit all United States citizens to their undergraduate programs without regard to family financial circumstances, other than those admitted from a wait list; and

   b) provide financial aid sufficient to meet the full need of all such students.

2. Participating Schools may agree to provide only need-based financial aid and to prohibit merit scholarships.

3. Participating Schools may jointly discuss and agree on principles of need analysis, but may not thereby eliminate all professional judgment on the part of individual financial aid officers.

4. Before financial aid awards are made, Participating Schools may exchange through a central computer facility data on commonly-admitted applicants regarding family and student assets and income, number of family members, and the number of siblings in college. Each participating school may retrieve each data only once for reach applicant.

5. After financial aid award letters are sent to students, each participating school may submit financial aid data to an independent third party for analysis. The independent third party shall tabulate and disclose the following to all Participating Schools:

a) For each pair of schools:

    (1) the total number of cross-admitted applicants who receive financial aid; and

    (2) the number of each cross-admitted applicants for whom the family contribution of one school exceeds the family contribution of the other school by at least (a) 20%, and (b) 50%, of the average family contribution of all aided applicants across all Participating Schools;

b) For each Participating School, the number of students, if any, for whom the sum of family contribution plus financial aid from all sources (1) exceeds, and (2) fell short of, the school's student budget.

6. Until the graduation of each admitted class, each Participating School shall maintain with respect to that class (a) all reports received from the independent third party, and (b) data consisting of the number of students offered financial aid and the number admitted from a wait list.

7. Participating Schools may jointly develop uniform applications for collecting data from financial aid applicants, but each shall remain free to request and utilize additional or different data from its applicants.

8. Participating Schools may not discuss or agree upon family contributions to be expected from individual aid applicants.

9. Participating Schools may not discuss or agree upon the mix of grants and self-help to be awarded individual aid applicants.

10. Participating Schools may not agree upon or exchange prospective tuition or general faculty salary levels.

Bibliography

Brookhiser, Richard, *Right Time, Right Place*, New York, Basic Books, 2009.

Buckley, William F., Jr., *God & Man at Yale*, South Bend Indiana, Gateway Editions, Ltd. 1977, originally published by Henry Regnery Company, Chicago, 1951.

Espenshade, Thomas and Alexandria Walton Radford, *No Longer Separate, Not Yet Equal*, Princeton University Press, 2009.

Harden, Nathan, *Sex and God at Yale*, New York, Thomas Dunne Books, 2012.

Judis, John B., *William F. Buckley, Jr.*, New York, Simon & Schuster, 1988.

Kelley, Brooks Mather, *Yale*, New Haven, Yale University Press, 1974.

Kendall, Willmoore, *The Conservative Affirmation*, Chicago, Henry Regnery Company, 1963.

------------ *John Locke and the Doctrine of Majority-Rule*, Urbana, University of Illinois Press, 1965.

------------ *Willmoore Kendall Contra Mundum*, edited by Nellie D Kendall, New Rochelle, Arlington House, 1971.

Kronman, Anthony T., *Education's End*, New Haven, Yale University Press, 2007.

Robbins, Alexandra, *Secrets of the Tomb*, Boston, Little, Brown and Company, 2002.

Soares, Joseph A., *The Power of Privilege*, Stanford University Press2007.

Sowell, Thomas, *Inside American Education*, The Free Press, 1993.

Vedder, Richard, *Going Broke by Degree, The AEI Press, 2004.*

About the Author

Edwin Rockefeller, a graduate of Yale College and Yale Law School, is a retired Washington, DC lawyer. He is a former chairman of the American Bar Association's Section of Antitrust Law and the author of *The Antitrust Religion,* Cato 2007.